Julius Shulman
Architecture and

Preface by Frank O. Gehry

Edited by Peter Gössel

TASCHEN
KÖLN LISBOA LONDON NEW YORK PARIS TOKYO

its Photography

Contents

Dedication

Dedication

My memories of childhood on a remote farm in eastern Connecticut remain vividly impressed in my mind. They form the very foundation of so much of my life. Even now, at the age of eighty-seven, the recall is founded on the stature and magnificence of my mother.

How was it possible for a young woman in the early years of this century to raise five children, milk the cows, feed the chickens, cook on a wood-coal stove, pump water from a well, obtain lighting from kerosene lamps, bathe five youngsters aged from a few months to the sub-teens of the two older girls, all in a tub on the kitchen floor next to the stove! We had no bathroom.

My love for my mother projected forcefully throughout the years. We arrived in Los Angeles in 1920 – I was ten years old. Our father established a clothing store where the family worked day and night. Father died in 1923, leaving my mother the gigantic task of managing a business, raising five children and for me, a blessing: of the five children I was the only one to live a private life, including seven years at university. Under mother's guidance and majestic patience, our family prospered; how fortunate that we had very few problems of conflict. I have never lost the precious reverence for my mother. She "understood" me, observing apparently that I was to make my own mark in the world. "Julius knows what he's doing," she uttered in response to my brothers' and sisters' protest that I was not required to work in the family store!

I was married in 1937, a year after my first "professional" photography. Our quarters consisted of a flat which served as my darkroom – Emma was fully cooperative, a loving companion until her death in 1973. As with my mother, she too abided with life ordained by work and the economy.

My blessings continued: three years after Emma's death I met Olga, a Viennese, who provided a richness of compatibility. To her I dedicate profound love and respect. We have been married now for twenty-two years. With our home and studio, a sanctuary in the hills above Hollywood, California, we live out our years, absorbing the constant demands for our photographs. But we maintain our vast "jungle" of our forty-year-old gardens.

My daughter, Judy McKee, provides me with earnest and structured assistance during her weekly visits from her home Santa Barbara. She has organized my studio so that it is a constantly renewed experience to walk in after breakfast to participate in her direction of a controlled work place!

All the complex labor of transcribing my hand-printed manuscript into her computer is handled by Susan Brandt. With utmost patience and skills she delivers "hard disks" to my editor, Peter Gössel, in Bremen, Germany. There he prepares mountains of photographs for publisher Benedikt Taschen.

To them I extend an endless volume of dedication. None of this would be possible without their warmth and personal involvement with my life's efforts.

Julius Shulman

First Church of Christ, 1959
Bernard Maybeck, Berkeley, California, 1910

Preface

Preface

When I met Julius in 1949, he was already a great architectural photographer. His works were already showcasing architects building in Southern California to the rest of the world. In fact, without him, that work would probably not have become so well known. Of course his talents were used beyond Southern California. This recognition was, and is, international. It's the Southern California part that I want to talk about.

I took an extension course with the ceramicist Glen Lukens at the University of Southern California. I was casting about, trying to find out what to be when I grew up, and I was attracted to art. During my time with Glen, he was deeply involved in building a wonderful house by the architect Raphael Soriano. Some intuition of Glen's led him to invite me to the building site one day, and he introduced me to Soriano. There he was, black beret, black shirt, black tie, sort of broken-nosed ruddy face. He was directing construction with great authority. I was terribly moved by this image. I found myself intrigued with the work of Soriano and the idea of architecture. I think it was Glen's hunch that would happen.

Wandering around the night school campus at the USC School of Architecture, I met a gentleman from Canada, Arnold Schrier. Since I was also from Canada, we became acquainted. He was studying architecture in a graduate program at USC, and he became a friend to whom I talked about architecture. At Glen Lukens' urging, I took a class in architectural design. Having a compadre like Schrier to play with, we traveled all over Los Angeles together on weekends looking at the great works of architecture by Schindler, Neutra, Wright, etc. It was during those excursions that I met Julius Shulman. Julius was in the midst of having a home and studio built by none other than Raphael Soriano, so I felt related already. It was in those early months of my first involvement with architecture that I discovered Julius to be a very generous teacher. He must have sensed the first stirrings of a future architect, and he invited Arnold and me to the site and to his house for dinner often. At those soirees,

I met many of the architects whose work Julius photographed in Southern California. Most notably, I became friends during that period with Craig Ellwood.

Those encounters, nutured by Julius Shulman, stirred my imagination and contributed a great deal to the beginnings of my career. Fortunately, I did well in that night class in architectural design, and at the end of the year, I was skipped ahead into the second year of the regular architecture program. During that year, before I started seriously into architecture, I was exposed to so much of what was going on in Southern California's architecture. All of my projects in that night class look like they had been designed by Soriano. I studied him well. As time went on, I was exposed to a whole other wing of Southern California architecture that came from Japan. A lot of returning GIs who had studied architecture were overwhelmed by the great beauty of the wooden structures they had seen in Japan and came back full of ideas that were easily translated into the wood frame language of Southern California building at this time. Harwell Harris was one of the leaders, and his work was extraordinarily beautiful to me. While it paid homage to Greene and Greene, and Maybeck, it struck out on its own and spawned a whole group of new young architects. Gordon Drake, Byles & Weston, Bill Rudolph and Cal Straub, who turned out to be someone who I would shortley meet, and someone who would have a great impact on my education as an architect. Cal taught my third year at USC. My third year was a turning point. I was totally consumed by the neo-Japanese language of architecture. It was so human and accessible, so easy to construct, so easy to fascinate about. I began to work totally in that idiom for my remaining years at USC.

During this period, Julius Shulman remained a friend and supporter. He encouraged me, even though the trends in architecture, in *Arts and Architecture* magazine, for which he photographed a lot of work, turned their back to me, and on Harwell Harris' wood language. Julius, in a great act of generosity, introduced me to his brother-in-law, who needed a house. I worked on that house in my fifth year of architecture school, in 1954, and needless to say, the

Victorian House
Los Angeles, California, ca. 1880

Steeves Residence, 1959
Frank O. Gehry, Brentwood, California, 1959

house resembled the work that I was emulating from Japan. I remember Julius arranged an interview for me with John Entenza to see if the design for his brother-in-law's house would pass muster with the old modernist. It did not. Entenza made fun of me and dashed my hopes. Julius continued to support the idea of the house, and it eventually got built. Not quite in the exact way that it was intended, but within reason, although in the end it wasn't for publication. Too many of the important details had slipped away, not controlled by the novice, which I was.

My next project, the Steeves House in Brentwood, evolved from the wood language that I was emulating, with a touch of Frank Lloyd Wright, which married easily to that idiom. Unfortunately, the Steeves House wasn't build by a group of craftsmen, it was built by a delightful old carpenter who left the dings on the wood as he pounded the nails. The aesthetic of the house, which needed a bit more craftmanship, came into being sloppily. It was the first project I collaborated on with Greg Walsh, one of my classmates. When it was finished, Julius generously offered to photograph it for us, which he did. He even managed to get it published in the *Los Angeles Times*, a great gift to a young architect barely out of school.

After the Steeves House, I was drafted into the army, and on discharge, I enrolled in city planning at Harvard Graduate School. It was there that I met the Europeans and fell in love with Corbusier. After graduation, I worked for Pereira and then Victor Gruen until 1960. I went off to Europe for a year to see the architectural history for myself. When I returned in late 1961, I opened my own shop in Santa Monica and started to explore architecture for real. Those years were very spare economically, as they always are. The thought of hiring a photographer of Julius' caliber to photograph our meager beginnings seemed improbable and impossible. I never bothered him. I knew if I imposed he would be generous, and felt that that was not appropriate. During these struggling years, I sort of lost touch with him. I would occasionally run into him at lectures or at architectural gatherings.

My early works with chain link and corrugated metal and plywood seemed contentious to everyone, although to me it logically grew out of the teachings of my mentors, Cal Straub, Garret Eckbo, et al. I found to my dismay that my teachers and mentors found my work distasteful to say the least, and they made known the fact they were curious about what I was doing but that they were rather sceptical.

I guess I lumped all of them together, and probably included Julius in the pile, and did not pursue further contact with any of them. It was like rejecting parents and moving on to my own world. It was normal, it had to be done this way. To the parents it seems rather ungrateful. Having children of my own, I've now been through it from the other side. Of course, I've lived long enough by now to have had students whom I loved and adored ignore me as they push into their own world. Fortunately for me and Julius, that didn't end it. Something happened. He called me, or I called him. We had lunch and I showed him what I was doing. This was very recently. My warm feelings for him from yesteryear came back to me in his presence, and he likewise opened his arms to resuming our friendship. The preface of this book is the result of that, and I am grateful.

Frank O. Gehry, February 3, 1998

Architecture and its Photography

Architecture and its Photography

This is my celebration of 62 years of the photography of architecture. I will embrace and reveal my abundant life's adventures with a camera throughout the world and 44 of the United States. Throughout my travels I have had the rewarding privilege of meeting and working with the giants of the design world.

The greatness of mankind is reflected in the created arts and architecture. Complementing the physical forms of this creativity are the inspired sounds and structures of musical epochs. The conductor and his instrumentalist can recreate the spirit and values of the composer, often with infinite sensitivity. Similarly, for the evaluation and study of architecture, libraries and book stores are filled with thousands upon thousands of volumes. They represent the expressions of critics, architectural historians, and countless numbers of other qualified "experts".

However, for the most part, those books, without photographic illustrations, would be vacuous. The photographer, therefore, assumes a role of tremendous responsibility in reporting, literally as a communicator. The mind, the dexterity, and the ability of the person with the camera can become the vehicle by which the image of architecture is transferred to the publications and people of the world.

How realistic is the critic in the estimation of the worth of an architectural statement – perhaps as recorded by a photographer? The thrust and validity of this question can best be demonstrated by reading a critique written by a prominent "expert" for *Progressive Architecture* magazine. He had written a review in 1977, when my newly-published book, *The Photography of Architecture and Design* was first issued. He stated, among other subjective "reasonings", that he did not accept "Shulman's over-corrected, filtered skies; that the reality of the scene (or structure) was not portrayed".

Showing architecture of a structure with the camera, according to his principles, indicated that our responsibility was to "show it the way it is". If the sky was murky or smoggy, no filter should be used to clean it up. If the sun on the building was non-existent, why not

Von Sternberg House, 1947
Richard Neutra, Northridge, California, 1935

15

photograph it anyway? After all, he suggested, the viewer is not concerned, for the most part, with aesthetics. He wants to see what is there.

How strange, nothing has changed! On page 13, in the above book, I wrote: "It must be photographed under the most optimum conditions possible." My contention has always been: the architect has involved himself, often for many months and years. Every line on his plans respects specific programming in his collaboration with the client. When the final statement is achieved and the building is "photographer-ready", the time has arrived when the structure can be introduced to the publication world. The historical value would be measured, as well as its role in the marketplace of clientele.

As evidenced by my own experiences over many decades, photographs become part of history and, therefore, the documentation of a structure must be such that the viewer of the photograph is first attracted to the graphic impact of the photograph. And then, in turn, the quality of the design becomes much more evident; it has an impact on the mind and eyes of the viewer., who can then form an estimation of it.

When presenting the results of an architect's design efforts to the world, it is possible that inconsiderate and immature-quality photography too frequently does not present graphic images. In turn, also, the publisher, editor or art director will dismiss the project even though the photographs may contain quality design elements. I have attended editorial discussions with magazine staffs in New York and observed the impact, or lack thereof, when packets of photographs are opened for review. Pursuant to the above, a statement issuing from one photograph may create immediate impact by its fulfillment of primary design expression. The composition and photographic qualities then combine for qualitative expression. Paul Goldberger, architectural critic of the *New York Times*, in reference to my photograph of Pierre Koenig's Case Study House (page 3), stated that the night scene represented an idealistic image of young people's dreams; what they visualized living in the hills of Hollywood, California could be – without ever having been there! This photograph has impressed all the architectural world and has appeared in practically every architectural magazine throughout the world.

A retrospective view of my career would at this time be appropriate, for certainly I could state that my cup of experiences runneth over. The question, what is the purpose of and what could be the direction that this highly specialized aspect of photography

will take? It can be stated that we literally translate a structure's design. The photograph can convey or create a mirror image of the subject. Or can the photographer take such liberty so as to transform? That could lead to altering, thereby affecting the form. The resultant exposure could bear a remote resemblance to the "original". In effect, a cartoon-like image could be created. In turn, even though the resultant image could possess visual drama, the photograph would not necessarily be of value towards projecting the architect's design intention.

Case Study House #22, 1960
Pierre Koenig, Los Angeles, California, 1959

17

Kaufmann House, 1947
Richard Neutra, Palm Springs, California, 1946

The above "transforming" process calls to mind an incident of the 1950s, wherein a committee representing a massive industrial organization in Germany, in search of an architect for their new expansions, were impressed by the publication in *Architectural Forum* of a project mirroring their needs. Arrangements proceeded. They met with the architect in New York, who escorted the committee to the project. What they observed did not portray the expected images as represented by the photographs in the *Forum*! The photographer had indeed, by the use of wide-angle perspectives, "transformed" the structure's physical proportions so drastically that the enthusiasm for the architect evaporated. Turned away by the impression, the committee cancelled its plans and returned to Germany empty-handed.

Whereas this dismal failure does not represent the norm, nevertheless it signals to the photographer: use thoughtful judgement in the creation of compositions. As suggested elsewhere in the following statements, the creation of a design impact can be achieved by adherence to observations of lighting, sunlight or artificial, on the subject of greater value than that gained by distorting forms.

My third mental gymnastic exercise in camera control of imagery can be labeled "transfiguration" – the process of idealization, glorification, and dramatization. Whereas we have evaluated two other processes of photographic interpretation, this third "exercise" does not involve optical manipulation, in which forms are varied in size, proportion or perspective according to the focal length of lenses. Certainly the twilight exposure of the Neutra house (page 96) could be identified with the term "transfiguration", or even glorified and dramatized. *Life*, which published the photograph in 1949, identified it with the latter term. Now consider the variations: the similar view of the Neutra scene in bright color (page 1) is quite adequate. If presented to an architectural journal as representative of the structure's siting and engineering features, it would undoubtedly have been published – both variations have been published throughout the years.

Kramer House, 1953
Richard Neutra, Norco, California, 1953

To further attest to the photograph's impact, in November, 1993, the *Journal of Architectural Education* published a 10-page article by Simon Niedenthal, an instructor at the Art Center College of Design in Pasadena, California. The essay portrays the various elements of the "history" of that "landmark" portrait of the house and how *Life* sought it for a story. Mrs. Neutra's comments are expressed, suggesting that even if no other photographs of the house had ever been taken, the twilight scene said it all.

Center of Design de Pasadena. Cet essai développe l'histoire de cette photo dans ses différentes phases – une « image de référence » selon l'auteur – et évoque la façon dont « Life » a élaboré son reportage. On y lit aussi les commentaires de Mme Neutra qui explique que même en l'absence de tout autre photo de la maison, ce cliché crépusculaire « disait tout ».

Même si la maison Kaufmann édifiée par Frank Lloyd Wright à Bear Run, Pennsylvanie, telle qu'elle a été illustrée par la célèbre photographie de Hedrich Blessing, a été copiée de nombreuses fois par d'autres photographes, ma vue de la maison Kaufmann de Neutra ne pouvait faire l'objet d'une telle répétition. C'est, écrit-il, la construction complexe de ma « proposition » qui en est la cause. Le même raisonnement, ajoute-t-il, s'applique à la vue crépusculaire de la maison Koenig. Elle non plus n'a jamais été imitée – si étrange que cela paraisse, je n'avais jamais prêté attention à ce fait.

Aux trois exercices mentionnés plus haut, à savoir traduire, transformer et transfigurer, nous pouvons en ajouter un quatrième : transcender. Ce terme me fut suggéré par mon ami Dan MacMasters, l'ancien critique architectural du « Los Angeles Times Home Magazine ». Dans une lettre, se référant à des projets auxquels lui et moi avions collaboré il y a de nombreuses années, il affirmait que certaines photos transcendaient littéralement l'aspect de l'architecture telle qu'on peut la découvrir à l'œil nu. En d'autres termes, la transcendance de l'image signifie qu'elle magnifie les qualités visuelles de l'édifice photographié. Sans pour autant trop solliciter l'imagination, cette démarche suppose de ne réaliser la prise de vues qu'après avoir dégagé et synthétisé les qualités qui vont produire le résultat photographique optimal.

Un jour, un groupe d'architectes hollandais me rendit visite après avoir visité la maison Koenig mentionnée plus haut. Ils me firent part de leur déception : la maison comme on le remarque généralement est une simple « coquille de verre audacieusement perchée sur le rebord d'une falaise » (c'est la définition de ma femme). La comparaison avec ma photographie les incita à mettre en question la pertinence de celle-ci. Nous eûmes une discussion très animée à ce sujet. Mon exercice constituait-il une représentation authentique et la photo n'aurait-elle pas dû plutôt être effectuée à la lumière du jour pour éviter la vision théâtrale qu'illustre la couverture du livre de Joseph Rosa ? Sans me laisser désarçonner, je sortis de mes dossiers un autre cliché de la maison, similaire à cette vue crépusculaire – quoiqu'effectué à une date antérieure dans un autre but – qui n'était pas une « vue construite ». Je

dois dire que ce document mit un terme immédiat à notre discussion. Mes invités furent d'accord pour reconnaître qu'une photo standard purement « quotidienne » de l'édifice ne représentait nullement la seule option possible. Un autre critique a affirmé que selon moi le photographe « devait créer des images subjectives ». Peut-être ce jugement est-il induit des 4 concepts énoncés plus haut et qui ont inspiré mon travail tout au long de ma carrière.

En réponse à l'opposition d'un critique à mes « ciels trop retravaillés et sur-filtrés », j'écrivis que l'architecture devait « être photographiée dans les meilleures conditions possibles ». Mais obtenir lesdites conditions est souvent malaisé et parfois impossible. C'est pourquoi j'ai eu recours à certains artifices : ce savoir-faire résulte de décennies d'observation de photos d'architecture. La meilleure confirmation de ces réflexions est apportée par deux photos : la première (page 23 en bas à gauche) restitue l'expérience visuelle brute. « C'est dommage »,

Maison Davis, 1960
David Fowler, Lake Arrowhead, Californie, 1960

23

Maison Hollander, 1962
Fenton Hollander, La Quinta, Californie, 1962

déclara l'architecte, « vous devriez voir ce site par un temps lumineux et dégagé ! » En utilisant un film infrarouge, j'obtins la seconde version de cette vue (page 23 en haut) initialement brumeuse et terne. Un grand format de cette deuxième version fut exposé dans une galerie où il suscita de vives réactions chez les visiteurs, professionnels ou non. Son impact graphique fut considérable. L'effet de neige poudreuse sur les sommets au loin est purement artificiel. Les effets d'eau noire et froide contribuent à créer une atmosphère particulière. Tout cela sans alourdir la facture du client, ce qu'aurait impliqué une deuxième prise de vue par un temps plus clair. Un film infrarouge de 4 x 5", telle était la solution. En ce qui concerne le pouvoir de l'imagination et de la créativité, regardez une autre photo de la maison Davis (page 23 en bas à droite). Elle a été prise pour permettre à l'architecte de mettre en valeur la structure du pavillon et la vue qu'on a de celui-ci. En étudiant la photographie, on a découvert que l'élargissement de la moitié inférieure de celle-ci améliorerait la qualité de l'image. C'est ainsi que la photographie agrandie suggère une ambiance magique, alors qu'au départ l'architecte avait simplement conçu le pavillon comme une sorte de belvédère.

On peut voir d'autres emplois de ce film infrarouge dans deux autres clichés où la composition devait illustrer les différents usages de l'espace du patio. Le rédacteur en chef d'un magazine de Palm Springs qui m'avait commandé cette photo avait décrété qu'il ne pourrait publier la photo « standard » à cause des contours brumeux des collines, que les visiteurs auraient tendance à confondre avec le brouillard de Los Angeles ! Dans le désert par un jour d'hiver normal, ils s'attendaient plus ou moins à retrouver la perfection glacée d'un dépliant touristique. Comme dans le précédent exemple, l'usage du film infrarouge permit d'éliminer la brume. Mais en outre, comme le film infrarouge fait apparaître les feuilles dans des tons clairs, les arbres et les buissons se détachent de l'arrière-plan de la montagne. L'aspect « plumeux » des feuillages ajoute à la puissance graphique de l'image.

Le moment est peut-être venu de discuter de ce que j'ai baptisé « acoustique visuelle ». Je voudrais revenir sur l'origine de cette formule. Le célèbre immeuble Bradbury a été construit par l'architecte George H. Wyman à Los Angeles en 1893. Il est passé relativement inaperçu pendant assez longtemps. Heureusement, au début des années cinquante la critique et historienne de l'architecture Esther McCoy me demanda de l'accompagner à l'immeuble Bradbury pour un reportage commandé par « Arts and Architecture ». Sa publication en 1953 a fait sensation dans le monde de l'architecture. Cet édifice

est devenu une mecque. Des visiteurs du monde entier accoururent pour rendre hommage à Wyman et à son audace créatrice. Comme j'ai eu l'occasion de photographier cette construction à plusieurs reprises dans les années qui suivirent, les étudiants en architecture, les historiens et les photographes m'ont souvent demandé : Qu'est-ce qui confère à l'immeuble Bradbury une telle importance dans l'histoire de l'architecture ? Je me souviens y avoir escorté un jour un groupe d'architectes. Comme nous entrions dans cet imposant volume, l'un d'eux, Harris Armstrong de St. Louis, s'est exclamé : « Mon Dieu ! J'ai ressenti la même impression quand je suis entré dans la basilique Saint-Pierre de Rome. Cet édifice devrait être classé ! » Il le fut effectivement au cours des années soixante.

Quand je me suis rendu au concert donné à l'occasion du centième anniversaire de Carnegie Hall, en regardant et en écoutant les plus grands musiciens du monde fêter cet événement dans une ambiance d'une telle perfection acoustique, j'ai songé à l'immeuble Bradbury. Pendant le concert, j'ai commencé à comprendre où résidait le secret du Bradbury : dans l'acoustique visuelle ! Où que l'on se tourne, de quelle façon qu'on y pénètre, on est confronté à une constante : l'expérience de l'espace est la même. Il n'existe aucun espace vide ! Ce phénomène visuel crée une sensation d'espace total. Sans recours à aucun stratagème, sans artifice d'aucune sorte. Apparemment personne ne sait au juste ce qui s'est passé dans l'esprit de Wyman quand il a accouché de cette extraordinaire construction. Il n'a plus réalisé aucun édifice important après le projet Bradbury.

Si je réfléchis à ma vie, les miracles de la photographie n'ont jamais cessé de m'émerveiller : je revois ces 62 années en segments qui vont et viennent, se fondent dans ma mémoire. De décennies en décennies, ces segments deviennent presque explosifs en ouvrant les portes de mes souvenirs.

Ils redécouvrent notamment les quelques milliers de photos que j'ai stockées dans mon ancienne chambre noire, des photos plus ou moins « oubliées » qui représentent souvent des réalisations architecturales remarquables. Elles avaient été effectuées à l'origine, dans les années trente, quarante et même cinquante, pour des architectes qui présentaient leurs créations les plus significatives à des concours ou à des publications spécialisées en architecture. La plupart d'entre elles ont été par la suite négligées ou rejetées parce qu'elles nous paraissaient moins bonnes que les projets en cours qui nous tenaient en haleine. Aujourd'hui, leurs qualités nous paraissent aussi évidentes que celles d'autres projets.

Immeuble Bradbury, 1970
George H. Wyman, Los Angeles, Californie, 1893

27

Mes commencements

Au cours de la première décennie de mon travail de photographe architectural, les commandes furent plutôt clairsemées. Je ne trouve que quelques noms sur mes registres de l'époque. Mais ce sont ceux d'architectes emblématiques : Richard Neutra (mon premier client), Rudolf M. Schindler, Raphael S. Soriano, Gregory Ain, J. R. Davidson. Leurs premières réalisations introduisirent aux Etats-Unis l'influence du Style International déjà largement répandu en Europe. Ces architectes sont tous décédés aujourd'hui, mais quelles images ils ont léguées à l'histoire de leur profession ! Les premières maisons que j'ai photographiées pour eux pourraient être qualifiées de « primitives ». Les années 1929 à 1936 n'avaient pas été tendres pour les architectes et leurs quelques clients. A l'époque de la crise, le respect rigoureux du budget était impératif. Compte tenu des difficultés rencontrées pour acquérir ne serait-ce que quelques accessoires, mêmes des rideaux ou des tapis, et des maigres efforts déployés pour aménager l'environnement des maisons, les photographies que je réalisais étaient souvent mornes. Si elles pouvaient satisfaire les besoins personnels des architectes, elles ne pouvaient guère, en général, prétendre éveiller l'intérêt des directeurs de magazine.

Quelques projets furent quand même acceptés et publiés : Neutra avait ainsi construit une maison pour Grace Miller à Palm Springs, Californie, en 1937. Pendant trois ans, jusqu'en 1939, Neutra et moi passâmes de nombreuses journées dans cette maison. Comme les saisons se succédaient et que le paysage s'étoffait, nous découvrions sans cesse de nouveaux aspects de cette réalisation. Mes photographies de cette maison ont pour la plupart été publiées et exposées à ce jour (tout récemment encore à Barcelone). J'ai conservé dans mes archives nombre d'observations pertinentes que formula Mrs Miller sur mes photos lorsqu'elle en analysa la composition. Il était providentiel pour un photographe novice comme moi d'entendre des commentaires aussi constructifs. En les relisant 60 ans plus tard, je mesure mieux l'importance des critiques – Mrs Miller n'était pas toujours favorable, mais elle restait objective, je dois le reconnaître. A la fin de ma troisième année de photographie professionnelle, je constate une amélio

Pavillon Ford à la California-Pacific International Exposition, 1935
Walter Dorwin Teague, San Diego, Californie, 1935

Maison Miller, 1939
Richard Neutra, Palm Springs, Californie, 1937

ration sensible dans la qualité de mes compositions et de mes épreuves. Le magazine « House Beautiful » publia une de mes photos de la maison avec le commentaire suivant : « La plus belle maison du désert d'Amérique du Nord ! »

Compte tenu de la modestie de ces premiers travaux accomplis en étroite collaboration avec mes clients, je ne pouvais guère imaginer leur importance future. Ces clients étaient aussi des amis. Nous n'étions jamais pressés par le temps, il s'agissait avant tout pour nous de garder une trace de leurs réalisations. Je n'oublierai jamais nos échanges alors que nous nous rendions sur les différents sites à photographier et la façon dont nous arrivions finalement à trouver la meilleure définition de la composition de l'image. Aujourd'hui, on me réclame sans cesse mes premières photographies : je trouve la récompense de nos efforts dans cette attention respectueuse aux réalisations des pionniers du modernisme.

En fouillant dans mes archives, je retrouve des projets qui ont connu un certain succès, ainsi ceux de Paul Laszlo que j'ai rencontré peu après qu'il ait quitté l'Allemagne et se soit installé en Californie.

Maison Buck, 1937
Rudolf M. Schindler, Los Angeles, Californie, 1934

J'ai photographié ses premiers projets dans ce pays en 1938 et 1939. Ces clichés furent publiés dans « House and Home ». Son rédacteur en chef, George Nelson, estimait les projets de Laszlo étonnamment compatibles avec le style de vie californien.

Dans les années trente, mes premières commandes en 1936 et les années suivantes furent réalisées avec un appareil Kodak « Vest Pocket ». La maison Buck de Schindler fut le thème de mon premier travail. L'une de ces photographies Kodak a été publiée en Angleterre en 1996 sur une double page. Elle est aussi impeccable et nette que celles que j'ai prises plus tard avec mes appareils 4 x 5". J'ai d'ailleurs envoyé au professeur August Sarnitz, conservateur des archives Otto Wagner à Vienne, un jeu complet de mes épreuves Schindler. Quand on les compare aux photographies plus tardives prises avec un appareil 4 x 5", les reproductions de l'ouvrage de Sarnitz consacré à Schindler apparaissent d'une qualité tout à fait équivalente.

Un équipement sophistiqué n'est pas toujours indispensable : je me souviens de la façon dont j'ai adapté mon appareil aux problèmes complexes que pose la photographie architecturale. Je n'avais à ma dis-

position qu'un seul et unique appareil, et je me rendais aux séances de prises de vue sans penser aux éventuels problèmes techniques qui pouvaient survenir. Quand j'ai visité l'exposition internationale de San Diego en 1935, j'ai réalisé par hasard un cliché du pavillon Ford, un édifice art déco. Je n'avais tiré aucune épreuve de ce négatif, mais j'ai quand même rangé la planche contact tirée du négatif dans mes archives. Des années plus tard, une conservatrice du Los Angeles County Museum of Art me demanda si je disposais d'un cliché d'un grand immeuble art déco. Je me souvins de mon cliché du pavillon Ford et lui montrai la planche. La conservatrice, qui avait besoin d'un agrandissement de 4,5 m de côté pour un accrochage mural, doutait que mon minuscule négatif soit utilisable. Je le lui ai prêté pour qu'elle le fasse examiner par un laboratoire. A la surprise générale, l'énorme agrandissement obtenu était extrêmement net. Quelle extraordinaire consécration de l'attention rigoureuse que j'apportais toujours au développement des films! Grâce à celle-ci, les négatifs obtenus étaient susceptible d'agrandissements infinis.

Cette anecdote illustre parfaitement la discipline à laquelle je m'astreignis dès mes débuts et grâce à laquelle nombre de photos prises à l'époque restent des documents si utiles aujourd'hui. Mes photographies prises à l'University of California de Berkeley en 1934 et 1935 sont toujours exposées et publiées aujourd'hui. Je suis surpris par la façon dont elles font ressortir les lignes structurelles des différents bâtiments du campus, car à cette époque, je n'avais pas encore décidé de me spécialiser dans la photo d'architecture.

Il y a parfois d'autres surprises qui surgissent de façon inattendue de mon cycle de photographies des années trente. Un jour, les nouveaux propriétaires de l'hôtel Shangri-La de Santa Monica me téléphonèrent. Ils avaient entendu dire que j'avais photographié la construction initiale, l'intérieur comme l'extérieur. «Auriez-vous par hasard conservé ces photographies?» me demandèrent-ils. J'avais effectué cette commande pour le compte de l'architecte William E. Foster en 1939 et 1940, et je leur ai expliqué que je possédais un album relié des photos de la décoration primitive. «C'est exactement ce dont nous avons un besoin urgent pour notre projet de restauration. Pouvons-nous venir à votre studio tout de suite?» Leur excitation quand ils commencèrent à feuilleter mon album vieux de 55 ans était à la mesure de leur surprise: ils n'auraient jamais imaginé retrouver une telle mine d'informations! Ils me demandèrent des nouveaux tirages. Les négatifs étaient parfaitement conservés. Pour animer ce décor, j'avais mis en scène une réception avec des figurants représen-

Ci-dessus:
Arrêt de bus à Wilshire Boulevard, 1933

A gauche:
Hôtel de ville, vu de la gare ferroviaire de Los Angeles, 1933
John C. Austin, John et Donald Parkinson, Albert C. Martin, Los Angeles, Californie, 1928

Hôtel Shangri-La, l'entrée et le hall, 1940
William E. Foster, Santa Monica, Californie, 1940

tant les invités, le tout avec l'aide d'un revendeur d'automobiles Packard, une luxueuse limousine de l'époque. Cette photographie crée une sorte de documentaire vivant.

En fouillant dans mes archives, je retrouve deux autres projets des années trente, ceux de Milton J. Black et S. Charles Lee, inspirés de l'esprit art déco dominant. Beaucoup des appartements si originaux de Black sont encore occupés à l'heure actuelle. Les cinémas au décor sophistiqué de Lee sont eux aussi encore en activité et commémorent cette période où les cinémas étaient imprégnés d'une atmosphère fantastique assortie aux films de l'époque, devenus aujourd'hui des classiques en noir et blanc.

A gauche:
Pont à la East 6th Street, 1933
Los Angeles, Californie

A droite:
Le cinéma Academy, 1939
S. Charles Lee, Los Angeles, Californie, 1939

Il est curieux de constater que tant de documents tirés de mes archives sont devenus des références importantes parce qu'ils représentent des lieux historiques. Ainsi cette photo prise en 1933, qui représente le chantier de la gare ferroviaire de Los Angeles où l'on voit la mairie se refléter dans une flaque d'eau, est l'une de mes photos les plus appréciées de l'époque où j'étais encore un « amateur éclairé ». J'ai réalisé beaucoup d'autres clichés durant cette période. Par exemple, ce détail de la structure métallique de l'arche d'un pont sur la Los Angeles River qui a été primé par un magazine de New York. Margaret Bourke White faisait partie du jury.

Certaines raisons techniques expliquent la qualité des photos de cette première période (à partir de 1933). Pour une raison dont je ne me souviens pas, j'avais fixé l'appareil sur un pied léger et ne prenais

Station-service, 1938
El Monte, Californie, vers 1935

chaque cliché qu'après m'être assuré de la stabilité absolue de l'appareil. De plus, comme je n'étais pas satisfait du minuscule viseur de l'appareil, j'en ai adapté un plus grand acheté au magasin d'articles de photo. Il rendait la composition de chaque scène bien plus commode. J'ai aussi utilisé un déclencheur souple pour m'assurer que l'appareil ne bougerait pas, surtout quand les temps de pose étaient longs.

En dehors de l'aspect purement « mécanique » de ma technique, j'ai observé au cours des ateliers et des séminaires que j'ai animés pour divers groupes et institutions que les étudiants négligeaient souvent les règles élémentaires de la perception. C'est pourquoi j'ai écrit en 1976 un article pour un journal de design : « L'œil perspicace ». Il a été écrit 40 ans après les débuts de ma carrière professionnelle. 20 autres années se sont écoulées depuis. Quand j'ai ressorti cet article de mes papiers, j'ai été enchanté par la cohérence de mes observations.

En 1927, j'ai pris une photo d'une « rencontre sportive » au lycée avec un appareil Brownie Box. Dès cette époque, la construction de la composition révélait que j'avais maîtrisé les paramètres de la photo avant le départ de la course de haies. En choisissant mon point de vue, j'avais veillé à ce qu'on voit l'espace qui se trouvait devant les coureurs. Je tins compte de la remarque de mon professeur : « Compte tenu de la vitesse lente de l'obturateur de votre appareil, le rendu des coureurs passant devant l'appareil sera flou. » Il était évident pour moi que l'effet de « bougé » ne serait pas aussi prononcé en photographiant les coureurs de derrière. Lors du cours suivant, mon professeur exprima sa surprise devant la position inattendue que j'avais choisie pour l'appareil sans m'arrêter à sa suggestion : « Vous aurez besoin d'une vitesse d'obturation élevée pour figer l'action. » Il n'était pas très compétent. De plus, comme il le reconnut en analysant ma composition, ce que j'avais exprimé dépassait la photo d'un simple « groupe de coureurs ». J'avais englobé l'espace en montrant les spectateurs, l'un des juges au premier plan ainsi qu'un autre tout au bout de la série de haies. Un mordu d'athlétisme a déclaré il y a quelque temps que selon lui personne n'avait jamais su rendre le sentiment total de la course comme cette photo : « Les photographes montrent toujours les coureurs enjambant la haie en plan rapproché. »

En 1933, j'ai reçu un appareil Kodak pour mon 23e anniversaire qui m'a accompagné dans mes balades exploratoires de Los Angeles. Mais à cette époque le projet de devenir photographe était bien loin d'avoir germé dans mon esprit. Je n'avais pas la moindre idée de ce que je voulais faire de ma vie.

En février 1936, après 7 ans passés à l'université, je n'avais pas trouvé de sujet pour ma licence. Je décidai que j'avais appris tout ce que j'avais besoin de savoir et que je ferais mieux de retourner dans ma famille à Los Angeles. Ma sœur, Shirley Baer, connaissait Dione Neutra, la femme du célèbre architecte Richard Neutra. Elle téléphona un jour à ma sœur pour lui demander si elle connaissait un studio à louer pour le nouvel élève de son mari. La réponse décida du cours de ma vie : « Oui, j'ai une chambre disponible à la maison, ce n'est pas très loin de votre cabinet. » Quelques jours plus tard, ma sœur me présenta au nouvel assistant de Richard Neutra. Un jour, il m'invita à l'accompagner : « M. Neutra m'a demandé de rencontrer un entrepreneur sur le chantier d'une maison qui est presque achevée sur les collines de Hollywood. » Cela se passait le 5 mars 1936. Pendant

Ci-dessous :
Dimanche matin à Mount Hollywood, 1933

En bas :
Course d'obstacles, 1927

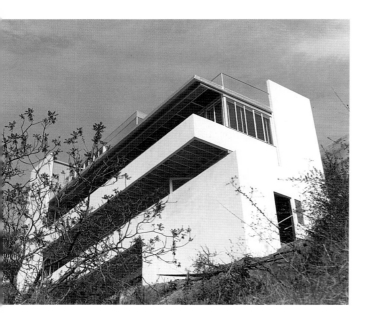

que mon ami discutait avec l'entrepreneur, je déambulais sur le chantier avec mon appareil Kodak « Vest Pocket ». Les 6 photographies une fois développées, je les envoyai à mon ami qui les montra à Neutra. Il me téléphona pour me dire que M. Neutra avait aimé mes photographies et qu'il souhaiterait me rencontrer pour savoir s'il pourrait en obtenir des doubles. J'étais ébahi, car je n'avais jamais rencontré d'architectes et la maison que j'avais photographiée m'intriguait avec ses formes étranges, elle était si différente des maisons que j'avais connues jusque-là ! J'ai accepté cette invitation. Neutra me demanda « si j'étais photographe ou si j'étudiais l'architecture ? ». Il avait beaucoup aimé mes clichés. Et c'est son invitation à réaliser d'autres photos pour lui qui a fait de moi un photographe. Cela après 7 années passées à l'University of California où je n'avais pas vraiment appris de métier. Comme si une puissance supérieure avait décrété que je devais passer toutes ces années à attendre ma rencontre avec l'architecte Richard Neutra. Non seulement il m'a demandé 6 épreuves supplémentaires des 6 photographies, mais il a également suggéré que je rencontre un architecte qui avait été jusqu'à une date récente son élève et qui achevait la construction d'une maison dans les environs.

Sur ce chantier, j'ai rencontré Raphael S. Soriano assis à même la moquette toute neuve du salon en train de déjeuner. J'ai partagé un sandwich avec lui, lui ai raconté ma rencontre avec Neutra qui le surprit. Neutra, d'après Soriano, se conduisait comme un tyran avec les photographes. Soriano me demanda ensuite si je voulais bien photographier la maison dans laquelle nous nous trouvions quand elle serait finie. Non seulement je photographiai la maison quelques semaines plus tard, mais la publication de ces photos aux Etats-Unis et à l'étranger contribua amplement à donner une image favorable de l'architecture de Soriano et de mes talents. Je me rends compte aujourd'hui, rétrospectivement, à quel point ce jour de mars 1936 a été déterminant. Notre amitié s'est renforcée dans les années suivantes, et j'ai photographié la plupart de ses projets de l'époque. En 1947, j'ai acheté un terrain pour y faire construire ma future maison et mon atelier, et je lui ai demandé s'il voulait en être l'architecte.

Quand je repense à lui, je ne peux m'empêcher de me rappeler un incident qui après 60 ans ou plus continue de me contrarier. J'étais assis sur un canapé de son atelier-appartement en 1937 et je venais de lui apporter des photographies. Il me demanda d'attendre avec lui la visite de nouveaux clients, un couple qui lui avait demandé de concevoir une maison pour eux. C'était une chance rare, car nous sortions à peine de la grande dépression dans ces années 1936–37, et les archi-

Above and left:
Kun House, 1936
Richard Neutra, Los Angeles, California, 1936

Overleaf:
Strathmore Apartments, 1937
Richard Neutra, Los Angeles, California, 1936

41

Lipetz House, 1936
Raphael S. Soriano, Los Angeles, California, 1935

all of his projects. In 1947, acquiring land for a future home and studio, I asked if he would design them for us.

It is strange, however, to recall earlier experiences with Soriano when we were both beginning our respective careers. There was one incident which, after 60 or more years, continues to upset me. I was seated on a sofa in his apartment-studio in 1937, where I had delivered some photographs. He asked me to await the visit of some new clients, a husband and wife who had asked if Soriano would consider designing a house for them. That was a rare treat because in those days, around 1936 and 1937, prior to World War II, our economy was just moving out of a disastrous depression and architects were fortunate to gain the trust of a potential client. Shortly thereafter there was a knock at the door and Soriano admitted a young husband and wife, seated them at his desk. I sat back and listened to their conversation, during which the wife extracted

44

from a bag a group of pages she had torn from magazines. Her husband explained that she was quite a gourmet cook and would appreciate in Soriano's design anything he could do to make her kitchen more useful and more versatile to accommodate her creativity in that field. As she proceeded to ask Soriano what he thought of some of the details in her clippings, he suddenly rose to his feet and, red-faced, shouted at the couple, "You don't need me, why don't you just get any building contractor and let him build what you want. I am an architect and I shouldn't be bothered with a person trying to tell me how to design a house." With that exclamation, Soriano walked to the door, opened it, and said to the couple, "Perhaps you had better leave." I have never been more embarrassed in my life. To sit there and overhear such ragged, disgraceful behavior on the part of a professional. I couldn't understand what happened because Soriano was a rather affable person, warm, cordial, and friendly. Afterwards I asked him why he had exploded. He suggested that they were trying to tell him how to design their house. I retorted, "Raphael, what makes you say that?" They were a quiet, polite couple who were serious in their intent, apparently affluent enough to be able to afford to build a new house in those poverty-stricken days. "They were not trying to tell you anything. She apologized, if you may recall, when she took out the pages from the magazines. She did not say this is what she wanted. I recall vividly her saying to you, 'Mr. Soriano, I would appreciate very

Los Angeles Jewish Community Center, 1937
the building site during and before construction
Raphael S. Soriano, Los Angeles, California, 1937

Fitzpatrick House, living room, 1937
Rudolf M. Schindler, Los Angeles, California, 1936

much if you could help me in the design of a kitchen which embraces some of these features which I have torn out of magazines.' That's as far as her request extended." Of course, Soriano realized how stupid it was for him to drive away a client. They were apparently an affluent couple, willing and able to trust Soriano to create what could have been a wonderful house. After all, in those years, if an architect had one client a year, he could consider himself as having discovered a bonanza.

On a recent walk down the path where I stepped in 1937 for my first meeting with Schindler, my mind responded with a glow of warm memories. Entering his studio space I had observed him seated at his desk, next to a warming fireplace. Nodding to a chair for me, he completed his telephone conversation. "There, I have just contracted my next house's construction." Of course, I had no idea what he was referring to. I knew very little of the practice of architecture in those days. "Now," he asked, "who are you? I understand that you are beginning to take photographs of architecture."

Fitzpatrick House, 1937
Rudolf M. Schindler, Los Angeles, California, 1936

I responded by describing my Neutra Kun House adventure, how it was the first modern house of its form I had ever seen and that Neutra was the first architect I had ever met. Further conversation resulted in my detailing how Neutra not only accepted all six of my Kun photographs but had also requested six each additional 8" x 10" prints. Apparently Schindler was impressed. He asked if I would photograph his recently completed Fitzpatrick House. Thereafter I continued with other projects for him.

My relationship with Schindler was a cordial one. Although he never attended an assignment with me, he provided invaluable critiques of my photographs. I particularly recall his comments when reviewing prints of his Daugherty house in the Santa Monica mountains. He asked: "Why on your interiors is the lighting equal in intensity on adjacent walls?" He then pointed to the naturally illuminated walls in his studio. Each differed, the light sources struck at varied angles. What a lesson! In my use of floodlights it had not occurred to me that illumination need not be uniform. Schindler's

Maitland Residence, 1940
Julius Ralph Davidson, Bel Air, California, 1940

observations were timely for, as I became more active, there was a growing responsibility for more realistic identity of natural values in my interior compositions. My photographic techniques were further enhanced by his continuing objective comments on my interpretations to his designs. We both gained.

There is another important name in my immeasurably prolonged chain in which names had become links which forged together those fortunate enough to have lived and worked during those pioneering decades. J. R. Davidson was a designer who arrived in New York in 1923, from Berlin. He settled in Los Angeles in 1925, where he embarked upon designing a series of disciplined, International Style houses. My association with Davidson began in the early 1940s, photographing his first house in this area. The Maitland residence involved remodeling an old Georgian mansion. I photographed it in 1940.

Herein lies one of the answers to frequent queries: quite simply I was at the right place at the right time. I was inclined with Davidson as with so many of my first architects' meetings to not impair our "business" relations with burdening financial matters. After all, during those formative years a loaf of bread would cost ten cents. I was willing to share my bread.

Davidson and his wife Greta became good friends. My wife and daughter visited frequently. Our Sunday morning breakfasts were delightfully rich in conversation. Contrary to the difficulty of the depression years of the 1930s and early 1940s, J. R. attracted a wide range of clients. His genteel manner and friendly disposition created an aura of trust among his clients. I recall a humorous situation wherein Davidson, in the course of detailing a dressing room, inquired of the client's wife: "What size brassiere do you wear?" She was taken aback, but his explanation was that his drawer designs encompassed dimensions required for specific garments. The question's surprise evaporated, and his thoroughness created a trouble-free happy client's home.

Fortunately, J. R.'s clients made my photographic life considerably relaxed. Most were favorably disposed to collaborate wholeheartedly with him and his wife in fulfilling their plans. Greta was an able associate, establishing close rapport with the clients' wives in determining space organization. That may seem to be irrelevant to many, but with my observations among architects, there were numbers of houses in which dissatisfaction arose: "I thought that the kitchen was not here but there"; and "It seems that (to the architect!)

Sardi's Restaurant, 1939
Julius Ralph Davidson, Los Angeles, California, 1939

you put the living room on the wrong side of our property." Davidson would frequently comment that Greta made his design communication successful because of her skill in relating specifically with the woman of the house. Sources of misunderstandings were thereby eliminated.

Furthermore, it was difficult for me to understand why Davidson had no problems with the landscaping of his projects compared to those besetting Richard Neutra. Perhaps that situation can be ascribed to the fact that the latter was impatient, often having me photograph before landscaping was developed – or even planned. Arriving at a location with his car loaded with branches of trees and cuttings from shrubs, Neutra immediately proceeded to direct his assistant to "plant" them. Very few of his early works were published except, of course, in those magazines, mostly in Europe, which were academically concerned with the theories of Richard Neutra's international style. In this country, editors refused to grace their magazines' pages with obviously misdirected landscaping attempts. An incident of this nature occurred many years ago with one of Richard Neutra's school projects which I had photographed. He had strewn many branches over the ground between the camera and the buildings of the school. Afterwards, on the finished prints, he would doctor up the images with pencil so that it would appear that the landscaping was actually a ground cover. Unfortunately, by stacking the pencil-retouched prints on top of each other, they arrived at the magazine office smeared and dirty beyond any possible use in the publication. The editor called me and asked, "Please save my life. Do you have any prints that Neutra has not applied grease pencil to?" Fortunately, I immediately mailed a set of clean, untouched photographs and the issue came out in time for the presentation as planned. Neutra never once commented that the publication in the magazine did not show any of his previously retouched photographs.

Those early years were invaluable for us: we worked together, for those fortunate enough to gain even one contract each year were able to spend time with me in the learning processes of creating photographs that would hopefully be published by professional journals. The work of those pioneers was eagerly accepted. Even editors were learning, along with us, how to select and present the

Dunsmuir Apartments, 1938
Gregory Ain, Los Angeles, California, 1937

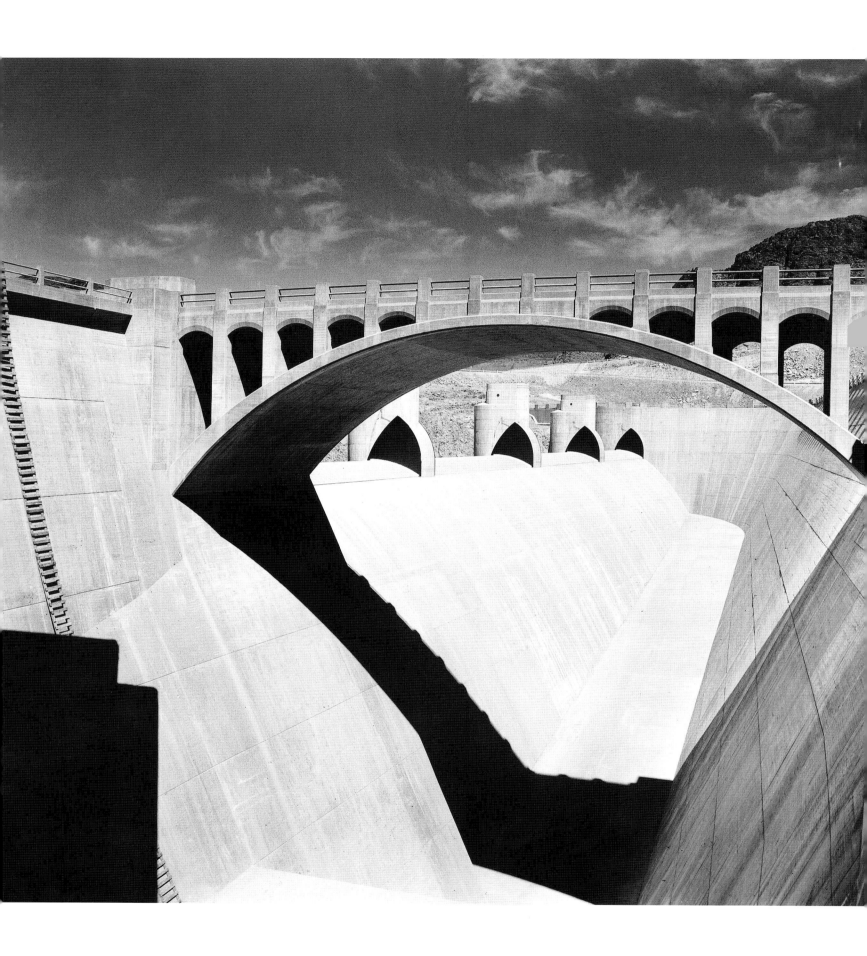

Boulder Dam, 1936
Bureau of Reclamation Engineers, Gordon B.
Kaufmann, Boulder City, Nevada, 1931–36

results of our "team" works. Gregory Ain's first houses impressed the Museum of Modern Art enough for them to commission him to design a house in New York on the museum grounds. It served as a demonstration of "workable and efficient" design.

Continuing recognition of the pioneers was furthered with the inclusion of some of their works in one of the first books on contemporary architecture, *The Modern Home in America* by Professor James Ford of Harvard University and his wife, Katherine Morrow Ford. They had seen my work in a number of current magazines, and were able to select a cross section of available designs for publication. So there again was a source of material which helped to publicize the architect's work and of course gave me nationwide and even international exposure for my photography. In 1947 I had the opportunity of meeting Katherine Ford, after I had photographed the home of architect Albert Frey in Palm Springs. By that time Mrs Ford had become architectural editor of *House and Garden* magazine. She and others of the editors, impressed by my coverage on the Frey house, invited me to meet the staff. On one of the evenings, at an event at Ford's home in Manhattan, I met a number of leading architects, including Walter Gropius and Edward Durell Stone.

My last major project, prior to a two-year stint in the United States Army, involved photographing the newly-constructed synthetic rubber plant in Los Angeles. *Arts and Architecture* magazine had given me an assignment in October, 1943, a few weeks before I was inducted into the Army in November. Los Angeles had been selected by the War Production Board as the site of a major plant for the production of synthetic rubber. The Japanese had captured most of the sources of natural rubber throughout Southeast Asia and the situation was extremely critical.

To photograph the project was indeed a spectacular event in my life. For at least 10 days I wandered throughout the vast expanses of the site – having been screened by governmental security agents, I was given carte blanche permission for full access to all areas of my choice. I recall this time, the "child in a candy store" thrill of the occasion. I worked alone, my 4" x 5" tripod mounted view camera and shoulder film accessories bag on my shoulders. It was difficult to restrain my excitement.

I used no lighting to supplement the existing protective fixtures. Many of the chemical products in the plant were highly volatile – I had been forewarned not to use other light sources. The assignment was open-ended: no prerequisites as to numbers of photographs nor delivery time. The weather was ideal. I received whole-hearted cooperation from workers and authorities. Using the former as "models" throughout the plant, they had been instructed to "wear clean clothing" during my "tenure" as plant photographer. Even lunches in the plant cafeteria were a pleasant respite. In conversations with the plant operators I learned much about the procedures and intricacies of production.

Together with an extensive coverage in Arts and Architecture, the major contracting firm with the three principal participants: Dow Chemical, Shell Oil Co., and U. S. Rubber Co., published a handsome brochure using an informative display of my photographs. The photographs, apart from that brochure, have been used for many of my exhibits and have been published in industrial journals. 35mm slides made from the original black and white scenes add to many of my workshop seminars.

During my two year sojourn in the army I worked as a public relations, special services, and post and surgery photographer. These photographs were used for the hospitals' reports on activities to the United States Surgeon General's Office in Washington, D. C. The surgery photos were included in a publication reviewing the progress of army surgery during war years. That particular photography in surgery every day for most of the week was a remarkable experience, for I had never been attendant to any surgical experience previously. Yet within a few days after being assigned to the hospital I was called to photograph chest surgery for the removal of a patient's lung. This was followed by several varieties of surgery over the course of the two years. I had a remarkably ingenious rack assembled for me by the army engineers where I was able to climb a ladder-like structure which was bridged across the surgery table, my 4" x 5" Graphic View camera bolted to the bridge overlooking the surgery table. An attendant working with me had a signal which could raise or lower the contraption, making it possible for me to get overall or close-up views of the surgery incisions. I would climb the ladder, lie on the platform created over the top of the contrivance, and by an ingenious arrangement I was able to focus and cock my shutter for each exposure. The compositions were determined by the surgeon, who would want certain aspects of the surgery recorded, and he

Synthetic Rubber Plant, 1943
Dow Chemical, Shell Oil, U. S. Rubber Co.,
Los Angeles, California, 1943

Hospital scene, 1943

would give me a signal. With a wink of his eye, the attendants would strip off the bloody towels and apply whatever was necessary to give me a realistic view of that phase of the surgery. I must say it was a delightfully exciting period of my life – not as exciting perhaps as the above-mentioned synthetic rubber industry plant photographs, but nonetheless a beautiful experience working with these great surgeons.

Apart from the surgical photography, I was also assigned to photograph for the special services department scenes taken on weekly bus trips for patients who were recovering from their war injuries and since Spokane, Washington was in the center of eastern Washington, there were many beautiful lakes and forests and mountains in the general area which was the site of our activities at least once a week throughout my two years. The photographs I took on those occasions were essentially of the patients' activities on the

tours conducted by the army and the special services department and public relations officials.

Though all the photographs taken during my service in the army were sent directly to Washington D.C. after my initial prints were made, I have no record nor did I ever receive permission to use any of the photographs other than for army purposes. However, I do have one photograph which I retained because it was taken at another army hospital where I was assigned temporarily to train a new photographer in the procedure in surgery. It is of a heart repair and taken from a little different position than I would have taken in my own environmental situation at Baxter. My public relations pictures of the patients are also illustrated in the same way – I had extra prints which I had from my own personal files so there again I was able to use them for illustrations here.

Shulman is Back!

Shulman is Back!

Discharged from the army in October, 1945, I re-established my studio-office in Los Angeles to prepare for a resumption of my career. Little did I anticipate what was in store for me. Apparently word got around: "Shulman is back!" Revival, although gratifying, was overwhelming. Immediately I employed two assistants; for in my first divided decade, 1936 to 1946, I seldom performed more than two or three assignments in a week. Working alone, I comfortably photographed, processed and even delivered 8 x 10 inch glossy prints between assignments.

One of the first assignments I did was for an architect who had designed a low-cost housing unit constructed out of aircraft components built of aluminum. With VE Day and VJ Day behind us in calendar cycles of time, some critical problems arose: what about the countless numbers of military workers throughout the country? And, with the cessation of military requirements and the return to civilian life of countless numbers of men and women, the absence of adequate housing created a crisis.

One such situation in an aviation plant in Southern California was resolved in a constructive and original manner. The company's officials, in conjunction with architect Edward Barnes, realized that aviation components could readily be converted to structure walls for housing, the demand for which was overwhelming in those postwar years by the numbers of returning GIs. A company official in conjunction with architect Edward Barnes and industrial designer Henry Dreyfuss, in their observations of the available facilities, soon designed components which could readily be adapted to wall construction for housing. I was asked to photograph, in complete detail at the plant, the process of conversion through to completed homes. When the designs were completed the company acquired a site on which to erect houses totally furnished and landscaped. My photographic assignment demonstrated the various phases of the above procedures, culminating with the photography of completed houses in the aircraft plant and thereafter illustrating attractively landscaped and furnished structures in garden-like settings acquired

Desert Hot Springs Motel, 1947
John Lautner, Desert Hot Springs, California, 1947

Prototype for Southern California Homes, Inc., 1947
Edward Barnes, Henry Dreyfuss, Los Angeles, California, 1947

for demonstrations. The step-by-step process of creating aluminum walled structures required my on-the-job learning of the intricacies of procedure. The resultant photographs have continued to be published, for with the closing of many military operations after the "cold war" period of the 50s and 60s, the need arose once again for critical employment conversion. National architectural and home magazines published the results of the construction techniques and the "ready for occupancy" pioneering efforts: war products into available housing.

I received additional assignments from national architectural journals and popular magazines. The illustrations of the construction techniques and the "ready for occupancy" ones are represented here. They demonstrate the broad scope of a photographer's responsibilities, for, as in most assignments, the reliance to produce editorial quality statements is essentially on our shoulders – or "on our camera's sightings." I did several assignments over the next one and one-half to two years for various publications and some of the photographs are still being used today.

Immediately after World War II, John Entenza, publisher and editor of *Arts and Architecture* magazine, embarked upon an ambitious program of designing and building a series of homes. They were intended to confront the problems of architects, builders, and potential clients during those hectic years of inflation, shortage of materials, and financing difficulties. Since the late 1930s I had been closely associated with *Arts and Architecture* magazine. Many of my earliest endeavors were published in its pages. Therefore with the first introduction of the program I entertained thoughts: this enterprise is of major significance and should contribute to the elevation of design standards among architects. It would constitute a hoped-for boost to living standards of low-income families.

With its idealized vision of post-war architectural progress, I was enthusiastic as were others in the building and design professions. From the onset of the earliest plans I volunteered to provide photography because the low circulation of the magazine garnered

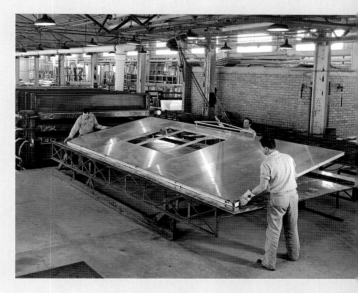

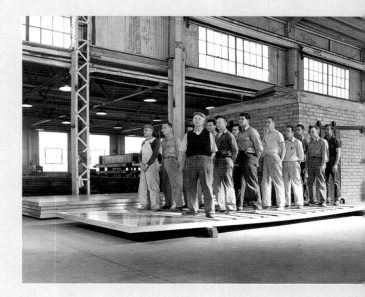

Overleaf:
Case Study House #8 (Eames House), 1958
Charles Eames, Pacific Palisades, California, 1945–49

Case Study House #8 (Eames House), 1958
Charles Eames, Pacific Palisades, California, 1945–49

minimal advertising revenues. Entenza proceeded to select architects whose designs embodied his personal preferences, omitting those designers not meeting Entenza's "rules": flat-roofed, modular designs and preferably of steel framing. In other words he precluded the choice of architects whose talents would more adhere to the original highly heralded "philosophy": a program of study – of experimenting with concepts of design and structure techniques.

Unfortunately Entenza disregarded the protests of a body of architects, enthused with the program but asking why certain architects were denied participation. They were referring to those whose social concern superseded the physical roles of architectural practice. Gregory Ain, as an example of those concerned with the prospect of housing which would fit appropriately into the hoped-for determination of the Case Study program, was disregarded by John Entenza. Ain for many years had attacked problems of construction and design, aiming at avoidance of redundancy of structure and planning procedures as pursued by most of the selected architects. I had admired and respected his intentions. He and an associate, Joseph Stein, produced a prototype house which entertained construction and planning concepts of practical and applicable techniques for low cost housing.

Another approach to "Case Study" interpretation was presented by architects Whitney Smith and Wayne Williams. It consisted of a unique interpretation of prefabrication. Their "Plyformium", illustrated here, predicated upon a methodology which entered into a system of practical, economical techniques. Apparently its unorthodox denial of accepted standards failed to appeal to John Entenza – it too was refused; as was another Smith and Williams departure from the "specifications" of Entenza: a client had inquired as to the feasibility of aiming in his newly-planned home at a departure from a low-ceilinged flat-roofed structure. The result was dramatically successful; it served to demonstrate that modern homes could be emancipated from the international style which had dominated the design world for a long time.

All the above critique of the program notwithstanding, I continued to support it, photographing fifteen of the eighteen constructed houses. In that group there were several which did offer some support of the CSH idiom. Pierre Koenig's two houses achieved considerable international publication. One of my photographs, on the cover of author Joseph Rosa's biography of my career, *A Constructed View*, became a "best-seller". Koenig, as a

Left:
Samuel Booth House, 1956
Whitney Smith and Wayne Williams, Beverly Hills, California, 1956

Below:
Model of the "Plyformium" House, 1958
Whitney Smith and Wayne Williams, 1958

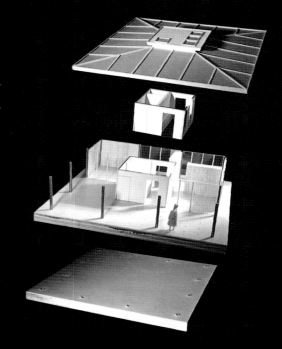

Case Study House #9,
(Entenza House), 1949
Charles Eames and Eero Saarinen,
Pacific Palisades, California,
1945–49

Professor at the University of Southern California School of Architecture in Los Angeles, has demonstrated the soundness of his disciplined designs. A newly-constructed steel-framed house confirms that.

Another successful architect of the venture was Edward Killingsworth of the firm Killingsworth, Brady and Smith. The Triad in La Jolla, California, consisting of three houses on a site overlooking the Pacific Ocean, offered choices of plans, siting, and appealing interior designs which served to attract much favorable response. Killingsworth also designed one of the most successful houses. In Naples, California, on a thirty-foot wide property facing a canal off an ocean bay, this compact yet spacious house demonstrated a close

Case Study House #21, 1958
Pierre Koenig, Los Angeles, California, 1956–58

Overleaf:
Case Study House #22, 1960
Pierre Koenig, Los Angeles, California, 1959–60

approach to the purposes of the program, in this instance, a minuscule property fully utilized.

A third participant team, Buff, Straub and Hensman, did two houses. One of them demonstrating the versatility of an all-brick house and maintaining an open plan also contributed to the program. The firm's barrel-vaulted roof design, the Saul Bass residence, succeeded in breaking away from the traditional flat-roofed contemporary performances.

With all the above fully surveyed, I am proud of my role in the production of the program. When the Museum of Contemporary Art in Los Angeles mounted a comprehensive exhibition of the program's essence, one of the most vital impacts – the scaled construction of a house by Minneapolis, Minnesota architect Ralph Rapson – demonstrated to the throngs in attendance one of the most appropriate designs of the Case Study House Program. Sadly, it was never built. After all the details were completed by Rapson, Entenza did not accept it.

The MOCA exhibition was accompanied by a comprehensive publication including a thorough essay on the entire history of the program. Unfortunately, although purported authorities presented essays, not one mention of my experiences or the facts of the program were included. This was because the writers were never involved as I was in the production of the project. At the 1940 and 1950 beginnings they were young people and most had never even of heard of John Entenza. But all was not lost. I continued to provide photographs to publishers who have sought as the best qualities of the houses built. Also *Domus*, in Milan, Italy published a special issue featuring its analysis of John Entenza's dreams.

Charles Eames, in 1974, agreed to write an introduction to my forthcoming book, *The Photography of Architecture and Design*. How grateful I was, for since 1950 when I had become acquainted with Charles Eames, when I photographed his Case Study House #8 for *Arts and Architecture* magazine, I was profoundly impressed by his demeanor. Here was a rare specimen of humanity, soft spoken and a genuine gentleman. Involved with a broad segment of the architects and others in the design world, I have encountered a varied "assortment" of personalities. I recall few individuals with whom there developed a feeling of warmth and closeness of expression in the course of our relationships. Therefore my memories of Charles Eames are treasured. In my estimation, I rank him among the "greats". Every project he participated in resulted in an expression of

Left:
Case Study House #23 (Triad), 1960
Edward Killingsworth, La Jolla, California, 1959–60

Overleaf:
Case Study House #28, 1966
Buff, Straub and Hensman, Thousand Oaks, California, 1965–66

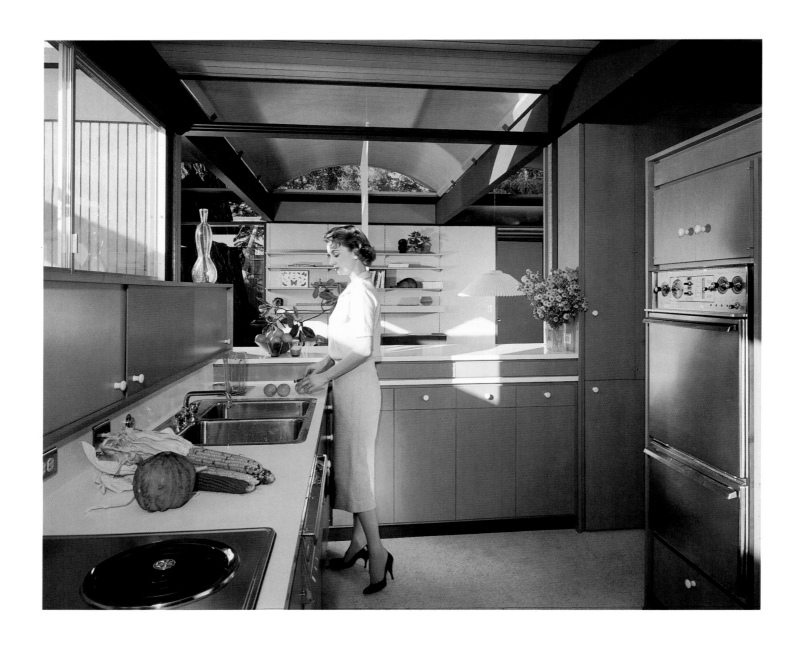

Case Study House #20 (Bass House), 1958
Conrad Buff, Calvin Straub, Donald Hensman,
Altadena, California, 1958

thorough, magnificent, complete statements about an individual's design or a quality respecting achievements of mankind. Tragically, Eames' rare abilities and talents were so forceful and demanded so much enthusiasm on his part that he literally destroyed himself with overwork. Once he started on a project, nothing in the world could disturb him in his effort to produce the most authentic and valid expression that he would be capable of contributing to the subject.

I recall the time when I was photographing his home, Case Study House #8, for *Arts and Architecture* magazine, and the John Entenza House adjacent to his, which Eames designed in collaboration with Eero Saarinen. Eames being a photographer by nature and talent had wanted very much to associate with me in working on both houses, but that never came to fruition because he was so involved in his workshop studio in another section of the city

that he never once came to attend even the taking of one photograph. I am genuinely sorry about this because there would not have been a greater experience for any photographer than to have the company of a man like Charles Eames to attend the workings of a photographic session.

Richard Neutra's community was a demonstration of how a perceptive concept became resolved into an informal, almost idealistic community of homes. During the 30s, Richard Neutra created his VDL House supported by the generosity and vision of Van Der Leeuw, a Dutch industrialist who was a strong guiding influence in Europe towards the development of significant structures to the most advanced designs by foremost architects of the epoch. In 1930, Van Der Leeuw, who had admired Neutra's designs and philosophy, gave Neutra a check for $ 3,000.00 as an advance to assist in the design and construction of what was to become an icon in the progression of architecture. The house became a formidable influence in terms of the public's exposure to the values and qualities

of life as demonstrated in the house's unique designs. During successive years, Neutra explored the land in the area south and east of the VDL House. He was drawn to a forested, rolling hills property overlooking the serene waters of Silver Lake, where he envisioned developing a community of homes in which, created by thoughtfully integrated designs, each domicile would experience unbroken views of the Lake.

The photographs which illustrate the evolution of Neutra's visionary "masterplan" demonstrate his sheer logic, the impact of his abilities and the keenness of his brilliant thought processes. From the onset of the far-reaching planning it was evident that the validity of the home siting would function in providing all of the desired qualities.

The first house of this enterprise, for Doctor Sokol, was followed by the Treweek residence. The two structures occupied sites along lake-fronting Silver Lake Boulevard. Neutra's concern with the inter-relationship of his houses is evident in my photograph. The melding of line and materials clearly portrays the logic of the interplay. Although a street divided the two locations, Neutra blended the Treweek interior with the Sokol house with a decorative stone wall which visually blocked out that street. Proceeding with specific photographic demonstrations of the effectiveness of the houses' siting, as it responds to the roof line of the house below it, vividly embraces much of the soundness of the entire community's development.

Treweek Residence, 1948
Richard Neutra, Los Angeles, California, 1948

90

Richard Neutra in his house on Silver Lake
Boulevard, 1963

The photograph with Neutra himself was taken during my extended
photography of the community. His favorite position while writing,
ensconced on a pillow, was directed towards his garden. Perhaps the
continual refining of the entire production could have been sparked
when Neutra sketched and wrote on his VDL House roof terrace. He
remarked during a conversation as we sat together: "God and Van
Der Leeuw created this blessing." His desire to share it with others
resulted in the "community" program.

A prime example, distressingly disregarded by those in pursuit
of information on contributors to architectural progression, are the
resourceful designs of Gordon Drake. Although short-lived, his
career was replete with international awards and publications. His
works continue to be published. The August, 1946 meeting with
Gordon Drake persists as one which generated an ongoing appraisal
of the potentials of a discerning thought process. Although by-passed
by many later generations, those who continued to assess Drake's
abilities and achievements were capable of enhancing their own
directions of objective architecture.

How rewarding was my friendship with Gordon Drake
following our first meeting in August, 1946. He had completed his
home on a lane in Beverly Glen Canyon in West Los Angeles. I
received a call: "Would you please come out to meet me and my
crew?" Most of those, calling as Drake had, did not ask "How much
do you charge?" Rather, as one architect described our meeting: "To

Drake House, 1946
Gordon Drake, Los Angeles, California, 1945

bring together kindred souls." It was more than that with Drake, for walking into the patio of his house, I was "just in time for lunch." I was introduced to his "crew," composed of a group of ex-marines in the Pacific area service with Drake; some others, a secretary, his girl-friend, two or three friends and associates. Those were representative of the past war years, ages in the 20s and a few in their early 30s – Gordon was 29. All were filled with enthusiasm, possessing a fervor to perform fulfilling architecture, inspired by the spirit of Drake.

My assistant had accompanied me to the meeting. After lunch we proceeded to plan our compositions. What an innovative design existed throughout the tiny house; the living room was only 12 x 8 feet. The entire house was built for $ 4,500.00! Accustomed to working in unrestricted spaces, I discovered that Drake's designs were so favorably interwoven that no matter where I looked, a revealing statement was evident. I sensed that here was one of the

most ingenious design assemblies ever to confront me; the photography of which was one of the most joyous and rewarding episodes of my then ten years of association with architecture.

That year, in August of 1946, marked the announcement of *Progressive Architecture* magazine's competition for "Recognition of architects attempting to improve contemporary standards." Drake's house was a winner, top award for his first house. So confident was I that when photographing a scene, from the living room to the patio, I placed on the table in front of the camera a copy of *Progressive Architecture* in which the competition was announced. Jokingly, I phrased to Drake: "My pronouncement – you will win first prize!" Not only was my forecast correct, but he was awarded 2nd place in the *House and Garden* magazine award in architecture in 1947. (Richard Neutra garnered 1st place). What a stimulation to me in my first decade of architectural photography, to become so eminent-

Trost House, 1949
Henry Trost, El Paso, Texas, 1909

ly associated with a man of brilliant expression, whose designs were not only functional, but adhered so favorably to his clients' needs. In succeeding time periods his work was published throughout the world, editors and architects proclaiming his designs: "As best to exemplify sound progress in design."

In March, 1996, the *Architectural Review* of London published a revealing article: 'Californian Promise' by Neil Jackson of the School of Architecture at Nottingham University. He related Drake's understanding of post-war technology to "a lyrical understanding of the California landscape." In retrospect, I am proud to have taken photographs which reflect and express Drake's short-lived career.

Gordon Drake died, age 35, while skiing in the Sierras in 1952. Neil Jackson and many others associated with the profession have observed that he was on the verge of becoming one of the great names in contemporary architecture. I miss his friendship, his care for others' lives and needs. He was a true missionary who sensed the urgency to fill the ever-widening gap in housing for neglected and disregarded minorities and so many of the minimal income populace. To the review of an indelibly impressed period of my life, I have worked with countless numbers of architects, but I recall none with the idealism and practicality of Drake.

The diversity of my assignments was realized in the course of performing for architects Carroll and Daeuble in El Paso, Texas in 1949. We were driving to a project when suddenly there appeared a house which I identified as the design of pioneer architect Louis

Sullivan. No, I was informed, Henry Trost designed it in the turn of the century years. My "schooling" in architectural history took a broad turn at that moment. Trost, I learned, from the 1880s to the 1930s, spanned a thriving career. His early association with Louis Sullivan and admiration of Frank Lloyd Wright in Chicago, with the advent of the Prairie School in later years, influenced El Paso designs.

Trost's exodus from Chicago to Arizona was followed by his developing a practice in El Paso. I was taken to see several of his buildings which I photographed for my collection of outstanding structures. His Mills building was perhaps the first ever of poured concrete. Worthy of historical recall, an article in an El Paso newspaper in 1954: "Henry Trost received his baptism in architecture during the Golden Age of the Chicago School in offices in that city, one of which was Adler and Sullivan where he worked beside a

Mills Building, 1949
Henry Trost, El Paso, Texas, 1912

brilliant young man, Frank Lloyd Wright, and under the direction of the father of modern architecture, Louis Sullivan." I recount the Trost schooling in my lectures to architectural students for it demonstrates how the linkage between architectural masters has evolved generation to generation.

It would appear that my involvement with the substance of architecture produced a marked impression on my photography. Through the 1940s I had become immersed in a disciplinarian mode of observing and recording the subjects of my assignments. My compositions displayed not only specific statements with a persistence to illustrate the interplay between spaces, but as one writer observed: "Shulman's extension of a building's siting almost to infinity furthers his requirement of showing where a building is situated." My preference, the Neutra Kaufmann photograph of 1947, with its projection of the structure, a penetration into the interiors and beyond to the infinity of the mountains and vast skies.

Richard Neutra and I had spent three days (and nights) in Palm Springs photographing his Kaufmann House. At twilight of the third day, I walked out to view the house from the garden – I had observed the "Alpenglow" of the developing evening twilight while in the living room and felt that this would create a scene of unusual impact. Running back to the house, I grasped my view camera and film bag. Neutra protested: "Mr. Kaufmann has been kind enough to take so much time in his home." He held my arm to restrain me – I broke free, ran outside and set up my camera. The result was one of the most widely published photographs in architectural history. As Mr. Kaufmann remarked when I presented him an enlarged print of the scene: "We should all be indebted to you for breaking away from Richard's grip on that fateful evening!" That especially after *Life* published a vivid statement about my photography, featuring the photograph. In recent years, as an example of the world-wide publication of this photograph, the *Journal of Architectural Education* published a 10-page article written by Simon Niedenthal of the faculty at the Pasadena Art Center College of Design. He presented

Kaufmann House, 1947
Richard Neutra, Palm Springs, California, 1946

97

Frey House, 1947
Albert Frey, Palm Springs, California, 1940

an intensive analysis of my twilight photograph of the Richard Neutra Kaufman house in Palm Springs, California. Since 1947, that scene has enjoyed one of the widest circulations of any photograph in the history of architecture.

In 1947, Albert Kornfeld, editor-in-chief, had been visiting in Palm Springs and had called me from there to ask if I would photograph the home of architect Albert Frey, who he had just visited the day before. He had spent a few days in Palm Springs just reviewing the architecture and was delighted to discover the Frey House, a tiny 16' x 20' box, but filled with delightful innovative ideas which he felt would make a good story for the magazine. "I would like to ask you to do a few photographs for a double-page

spread." Of course, I scheduled the assignment within a few days and when I met with Mr. Frey at his house I realized that herein lay a wealth of details which certainly fill more than the two pages offered by Kornfeld. There was no problem for me to spend the extra time with Mr. Frey. He was a delightful host and very cooperative in helping me produce the photographs which eventually were published worldwide. Within two weeks House and Garden magazine received in New York no fewer than 24 photographs, impressing Kornfeld and Katherine Morrow Ford, architectural editor to the extent that instead of two pages a six-page layout was published. After all, as I noted in a cover letter with the photographs, "This tiny house (16' x 20') possessed innovative ideas which could

Shulman House and Studio, 1950
Raphael S. Soriano, Los Angeles, California, 1950

be of much value to young post-WW II home builders, beginning with a similar space budget." As above, the six pages were enthusiastically accepted by House and Garden's readers; Mrs. Ford invited me to New York to meet the editorial staff and for a reception at her home. Were I abiding by Kornfeld's "two-page layout suggestion," I would have most likely not attained such a significant role in the photography work that I did for House and Garden magazine. I continued thereafter to produce assignments for House and Garden throughout the western United States for many, many years. The editors were chiefly concerned with landscape architecture, kitchen and home ideas, decorating, as well as the architectural department of the magazine, for which I produced many total home idea stories. The latter were mostly self-generated by my committing architects to give House and Garden first publishing rights on their better designs.

To add to the phenomena of March, 1936, our developing association led to my selection of Soriano, in 1947, as the architect to design my home and studio. I had acquired a large parcel of land in the hills above Hollywood, California. Construction began in May, 1949. My wife Emma, four-year old daughter Judy, and I moved in on March 5, 1950 – fourteen years to the day from my 1936 life's episode. An unexpected bonus was thrust into our lives: Soriano was the foremost pioneer in designing steel-framed structures in his world of architecture. How fortunate for us, for during successive decades, seismic activity left us untouched. Our home and studio were declared a Los Angeles Cultural Heritage Commission monument in 1987, as the only unaltered Soriano steel-framed structure of the many he designed and built during the years of his career.

As I remarked in a letter to Soriano of December 29, 1978: "Our home seems to accelerate in spirit and excitement as the years pass by. We finally have the living area especially, furnished in a most friendly and enveloping manner. The garden is even more exciting for Olga has transformed it into a flowery retreat. The above added to the density of our jungle of trees makes this home in my estimation the most complete in every respect. Of course, that is particularly so because we use it twenty-four hours a day. We are

home at least four to six days each week so you can imagine how indebted we are to you for having made it possible; a rare feat for an architect. I say that because with the passing years I truthfully have seen very few complete homes. So much is done for architectural trickery or the decoration is an obvious attempt to gild or to impress people and too often the gardens are manicured and stiff, formal statements."

My letter expresses much of my feelings about Soriano's sensitivity and ability to create what today is our haven of a glorious life. Walking into the studio adjoining our home, transports me into my world of 62 years of architectural photography of architecture. Sitting at my desk, the reverence for Soriano is almost overwhelming as I view the gardens through a 30-foot wall of glass. And scanning the surrounding studio spaces, totally immersing me with countless images reflecting a life's participation within the realm of the architectural profession, I cannot begin to express my gratitude for 48 years in this Soriano-created sanctuary.

Shulman House and Studio, 1950
Raphael S. Soriano, Los Angeles, California, 1950

Public Relations for Architects

Public Relations for Architects

Immediately after World War II, magazines and book publishers worldwide were searching for material to fill their pages. Television had not as yet gripped the media economy. Magazines were voluminous and together with burgeoning advertising pages, the marketplace for architectural photography was filled with heretofore unheard-of demands. The 1950s decade was one of the most productive in publication history.

A new source of assignments was generated when photographing a major structure which was slated for publication; advertising executives required product illustrations. I had become known among many industry advertising managers and their agencies. I referred to those as my "boiler room" accounts. Soon I was taking editorial quality photographs of equipment: heating boilers, water softener and air conditioning machinery, pumping installations, and toilets – I became humorously labeled, Crane Company's Urinal Specialist, because of my dramatically spot-lighted scenes. The photographs were used in widespread advertising programs: brochures, catalogues, trade shows, and journals. Many of the photographs were admired by editors as part of a structure rarely illustrated. "After all," I stated to editors, "why not show the 'guts' of a hospital for example? That is where every 'operation' is begun; is depended upon for complete services. The scenes are often most photogenic." So great were the number of requests, I had to devote at least two additional days to fulfill the coverage. Financially my compensation far surpassed editorial payments.

I was engaged with assignments for all the above in a wide ranging span of states, throughout the Midwest, New England, Texas, New Mexico and Arizona, the Pacific's Northwest area of Washington, Oregon, Idaho and into Montana to the East. The reason for my expanded travels: architects, new as well as older firms, were experiencing difficulty in obtaining quality photographs of their expanding roles. The post-war period generated architectural commissions for every conceivable building type, from minimal mass housing to luxurious mansions to complexes of huge apartments and

Horton Residence, 1961
Harold W. Levitt, Bel Air, California, 1960

105

American Airlines Jet Operational and
Maintenance Building, 1959
Coston, Frankfurt and Short, Tulsa, Oklahoma,
1959

ultimately including the then newly-accepted condominium concept. Schools, churches, libraries, hospitals and on and on! Not to overlook, of course, huge industrial complexes. I traveled throughout the country and into Europe, Mexico, South America, and of course Canada. The volume of my assignments, although originating in the 1940s period of my career, accelerated during the 1950s.

I recalled during my archival research of long dormant files, how primitive were the early attempts of architects to "dress" interiors or exteriors for photography. That was particularly evident during the waning years of our depression era. Those who by 1936 could afford to build a house had, in most instances, no funds except for barest minimal needs. Rudolf Schindler, for example, had me photograph his Pressburger residence during those years. The house

cost $ 7,500.00 and required a good part of a year to design and construct. I still wonder: what fee, if any, was paid to Schindler?

Not given to blunt pursuits of publicity, Schindler nevertheless was respectful of accurate communication of his work. He demonstrated to me how distorting a view could be if the angle of a camera's eye created an effect which denied his sense of proportion. This was similarly evident in his concern for transmission of light between two non-related areas. That facet of his sensitivity became clear to me while photographing his Erlik House in the 1954. While evaluating my completed assignment, I asked Schindler how he became alert to the visual relationship between rooms or areas. "On close scrutiny of my plans long ago, I observed that in a living area with a glass-walled orientation, the adjacent walled-in room could gather some of the abundant light simply by not allowing the

Erlik House, 1954
Rudolf M. Schindler, Hollywood, California, 1951

separating wall to the adjacent space to rise to the ceiling. Why not gain the required privacy with a governed height; then the remaining height could be achieved with glass – depending upon the total height of the ceiling." This particular device is well illustrated in one of my Erlik photographs, presented here.

Schindler's "light transmission," a brilliantly useful element in many of his designs, was not recognized as broadly as I felt it should have been. I wonder if light transmission meant much to other architects or to writers. Capturing light and expanding visual values are representative of a richness of total design. For me, the unique interplay offers an expanded experience in expressing architecture with photography. Curiously Neutra expanded his spaces, not as Schindler did, but by his use of mirrors which doubled a space.

Finally, an added dimension of feeling: Schindler's clients loved him for his genuine, warm-hearted Viennese charm. At the memorial service held after his death, there was not a dry eye among the scores of women attending the tribute to a great architect!

I have observed in my assignment log books that during those years, through the 1950s and 1960s, I completed four and frequently five projects in one week. I have rediscovered many superlative designs by architects, either forgotten, denied, or deceased. For this segment of my expressions I have selected works which even under today's design standards rate highly in my estimation. Planning was excellent and interior designs and landscaping were superlative. Apparently those pioneers were expressing thoughtful adherence to a discipline; a respect for clients' programs and to the relationships of site and orientation for a fulfillment of function, be it a home or school, neighborhood bank, or library.

I have had more than my share of accolades during the six decades of my career. Success and security have not warped my intention nor my continuing drive towards "spreading the Gospel." I react with disgust at the pages upon pages devoted in books and magazines to the so-called innovative "new" structures by the heroes among present day achievers. But if writers, editors, and publishers had the temerity (guts, if you will) to observe if their heroes could hold a candle against the genuine heroes in my lifetime, perhaps they would perform a much needed and hungered-for role in reflecting the true essence of architectural information and education.

For years now I have pleaded with writers of "new" books: please stop requesting permission to re-publish the works of previously accepted milestones. How many times should Frank

Lloyd Wright's Falling Water be commemorated? Surely Richard Neutra's contributions to architectural history are significant, but how many books have been published to remind us of the greatness of his Lovell house? I can conclude, accordingly, on reviewing my abundant archives that we have collectively neglected the recognition of the true history of contemporary architecture in this world, that we pay too much homage to current works and in turn lose sight of the historical and design contributions of past decades.

In view of this neglect I must recount a recent experience. I had extracted from my archives the pages of the *Architectural Forum* magazine of 1957, in which they produced a thorough multi-page article on "A New Approach to Environment." This pertained to a building which I had photographed in Albuquerque, New Mexico, in the 1956 period. It was a high-rise office building by architects Flatow and Moore and it was one of the first so-called revolutionary solar energy and heat pump principles applied to office buildings providing low cost heating and cooling. The article headline stated, "The consideration of controlled environment as an integral part of structure offers new vistas in the architecture of human comfort." What I found to be most revealing was the fact that the principles involved would be as pertinent today as they were so many years ago. One wonders why in the process of architecture and education we do not refer to historical facts more often, rather than trying to create so-called new approaches to situations for which the solutions were found so many decades ago. The purpose, therefore, of these pages is to alert students particularly to learn and study methods which were proven and applied so effectively. The article in *Architectural Forum* magazine represented a thorough treatment. On reading it now one could really observe that the information would be as valid today as it was in 1957.

On researching my archives for this autobiography, I realized that my role as a photographer throughout the country began with most of the architects, also in their early years of building up a constructive practice in their communities. For example, in Wichita, Kansas, the firm of Ramey and Himes; Crites and McConnell of Cedar Rapids, Iowa; Blaine Drake of Phoenix, Arizona; and, Don Polsky of Omaha, Nebraska. These above randomly selected architects were typical of my expanding career throughout the country. They had all called me at various times seeking out my "expertise" in creating innovative statements about their hard-won successes. In my work, extended the photographic process by considering, for ex-

Simms Building, 1956
Flatow and Moore, Albuquerque, New Mexico, 1955

111

ample, how the architect can utilize the photograph not only to mirror his design statements but also to publicize the client and the function of the structure. Photography can enhance a building's image by producing a graphic impact. It can address the development of an architect's personal influence and an organization's role in the creation of a statement that echoes the designs as well as the marketing values built into the organization of spaces, product displays, the standards of comfort enjoyed by an occupant of the facility.

During my many assignments in the Midwest states, I found that it was a logical function for me not only to take "pretty pictures," but to further the process along the path of image building. The client, in reality, is brought into the project. The overall appraisal of the architect-client association can produce dividends of a nature not evident during the building's evolution. This reminds me of another Midwestern assignment, one of my very first. I had received a call at my Los Angeles studio in the month of May. It was from the architects Ramey and Himes. They asked if I could do some photography of their work in Wichita, Kansas, and, as Cliff Ramey stated: "Help put us on the architectural map." He referred to numerous publications he had seen of my work. A few weeks later there was a meeting in Wichita. In reply to my first question I was informed that the official had friendly relations with one of Wichita's most prominent newspaper editors." A luncheon meeting was arranged for the next day. We spent the remaining hours of the day on a tour of the various projects to be photographed. The information gained was valuable for our next day's meeting; I had observed that a church on the tour was of a design quality suitable for one of my magazine contacts, and for a building magazine, also in New York, a small family house of an excellent plan offered an innovative potential.

At our newspaper meeting the next day I suggested that this was a favorable time in which to expose good designs to magazine editors. It would come as a surprise to them that the Midwest did not consist only of corn-fed cattle and miles upon miles of soybean, corn and wheat fields; that in the post-war years there had been a resurgence of urban energies. The architecture being erected was sure proof of this. What was more, the National Association of Home Builders, in Washington, had selected Wichita as the site of the next year's annual exposition, and I learned that all the eleven builders' proposed houses were to be designed by architects personally selected

112

by each of the builders. I immediately called a friend at *House and Home* magazine in New York. As editor-in-chief he commissioned me to produce a major coverage of this milestone project. With that news, and Ramey and Himes as one of the selected firms of architects, the editor realized the significance of a feature which appeared full page on the following Sunday.

The news of my presence in Wichita, that of Ramey and Himes having their current work published nationally, plus the endless editorial features the editors could produce about the forthcoming exposition of builders' houses and a readership increasingly aware of good architecture, all combined for an imposing message. I had volunteered to allow the newspaper photographers to observe my

National Association of Home Builders Model Home, 1954
Ramey and Himes, Wichita, Kansas, 1954

113

Adams School, 1961
Crites and McConnell, Cedar Rapids, Iowa, 1961

photography sessions at each house. Product photographs were likely to be off-beat for newspaper photographers. Providing illustrations for the potential advertisers, they would then be more editorial in concept. Among people in the architectural profession there was an understanding of good public relations; the antiquated *mores* which had previously prohibited public relations activity were no longer valid. Everyone gained substantially in our combined efforts. Finally, *House and Homes* production of the National Association of Home Builders home show was enormous. It featured a cover and numbers of informative editorial pages.

Another fulfilling experience occurred with architects Crites and McConnell in Cedar Rapids, Iowa. We met when they were students at the School of Engineering, Iowa State University, Ames, Iowa. They had attended a lecture/workshop I had been invited to produce in 1955. A continuing conversation revealed their plans, after that year's graduation, to open their firm in Cedar Rapids, Iowa: "Would you help us with the photography of our work? – when, of course, we get clients!" The ensuing years during the 1950s produced a remarkable program of collaboration between their work and my photography. There was no question about the quality of the design of these two young architects, for wherever I aimed my camera the resultant photographs seemed to create a tremendous impact among the viewers and also, of course, among the magazine editors in New York who had seldom observed any work of merit coming out of that part of the country.

One specific example occurred during this period, when I had photographed seven projects for the firm in various parts of the state of Iowa. Expecting to continue my travels into New York, where I had meetings with architectural magazine editors, I had my negatives processed and brought the approved prints with me to that city, where, after a meeting with the architectural editors of *House and Home* magazine, we earned a tremendous publication – all seven of the projects were reproduced in an ensuing issue of the magazine. Even *Life* magazine published a story about the success of the firm. As I laid out all of the proof prints on a conference table in their offices, one of the executives asked, "Well, Julius, let's see what you're bringing back from the land of the tall corn!"

The firm continued their successful career. On one memorable occasion, they won practically every prize during an award program for the Iowa State American Institute of Architects Chapter. The architects had submitted a broad cross section of their work which I had been photographing the previous year. During the presentation of the awards, one of the architects present rose to his feet and stated loudly for all to hear, "I don't believe it was fair of Crites and McConnell to introduce in their presentation such a large photograph as the one that received the major award." It was a 30" x 40" color print of one of their schools. This exclamation created an uproar among the architects attending the banquet, for no one had ever expected an architect to protest about the size of an award-seeking photo. After all, there was no previously proclaimed limit on how large a print could be. It so happened that this particular design was so far afield from the average work of the commercial architects in Iowa that it actually shocked a number of the old-time firms.

While photographing the work of architect Blaine Drake in Phoenix, Arizona in 1950, I was asked if I would like to meet Frank Lloyd Wright at nearby Taliesin West. A phone call and arrangements were completed. Drake had resided at Taliesin West for eight years as an aspiring young architect. He also had been Wright's driver during the season's changings – between Taliesin and Spring Green, Wisconsin. The following morning I was introduced to the Master. He extended permission to me to roam about freely with my 4" x 5" view camera. But first, he escorted me through the "camp", introducing me to the apprentices in the drafting room and others.

I had many conversations with Wright during the ensuing week, discussing my specialty of photographing architecture. My broad knowledge of current architecture and my acquaintance with scores upon scores of architects throughout the nation and numbers abroad as well, seemed to arouse his curiosity. I was surprised by his questions, particularly having realized that he was mostly a very private individual. The gist of his queries had to do with the relationship between architects and their clients, as if to compare notes, not necessarily to deter clients from their personal program needs but perhaps to avoid wasting time- and energy-consuming discussions. I commented: "Mr. Wright, in discussing personalities at meeting and conversations, I was given to understand that you were a belligerent, angry person. But having experienced a few short days of your presence, I observe that you are a congenial, objective person." He smiled, and stated: "I know, I am belligerent, angry,

demanding, derogatory and an obstinate person." Continuing, he suggested, "You are a young man, perhaps never been exposed to the whims or misstatements of experts. That will no doubt come later in your life. But with my characteristics, I am certain that not any of them were uttered by one who had ever met me. Most opinions are hand-me-downs, gleaned from others. But our society is structured upon a narrow base of prejudices. Therefore being opinionated is a convenient weapon for attacking one's imagined adversaries."

By the end of my week's visit our exchanges had become more personal – I suspected that Wright had seldom related with others as we did; that our spontaneous bond resulted from a smooth-flowing stream of objectivity. Spending my early mornings and late afternoons trying to observe and photograph elements of Taliesin's designs, I was prepared to comment or question during our conversations. I particularly would try to acquire information to further

Taliesin West, 1950
Frank Lloyd Wright, Scottsdale, Arizona, 1938–42

Taliesin West, 1950
Frank Lloyd Wright, Scottsdale, Arizona, 1938–42

my own enlightenment, and understanding: why were there so many "schools" of design among architects? I had never heard of such questions being brought to Wright's attention, but apparently he seemed to delight in my naivety. Our meetings were short but rich in context. There have been endless numbers of volumes dedicated to the creative genius of the man, but hardly ever have I read of the values which were expressed in our conversations. On departing, I asked Wright if he would like to review my week's photography. "Yes, I would like that very much," he responded.

What Wright expressed in his letter to me, dated July, 1950, sums up his feelings: what a thrill of gratification charged through me when I was asked by Wright to "do" his V.C. Morris shop in San Francisco. He made the necessary arrangements with the owner. When I presented my photographs on the completion of the project, another rewarding reaction from Wright was forthcoming. Seated at a table studying my photographs, he came upon one which apparently impressed him. He glanced at the print, at me, and back to the print. He arose, stepped around towards me. As I left my chair, to my surprise, he swung an arm around my shoulders: "Shulman," he exclaimed, "at last someone understands, in a photograph, my statement – you have penetrated the spirit of my design!" He was referring to my exterior detail of the arched brick entry to the shop. I had placed small spotlights on interior positions to back-light the arched entry area. An additional lamp was used to illuminate the visible background's display wall, balancing the visual qualities of the composition. He continued his comments: "I have seen numerous photographs which failed completely to express that design." In succeeding years, responding to requests from publishers and historians, I often included the above scene. Was it likely that Wright and I evaluated the properties of that statement in a special manner? Few recognized our favorite view of V.C. Morris.

During the 1950s, I photographed Wright's houses in Southern California in which he had developed his textile concrete block as the basic material. Those assignments of the Freeman, Ennis and early Storer compositions were performed with architectural writer and historian, Esther McCoy. Those photographs combined with extensive work on the Hollyhock house at a later date provided almost continuously, material on those Wright structures for publications throughout the world.

I have frequently been asked what differences have struck me in photographing such diverse designs as Neutra and Frank Lloyd

V. C. Morris Gift Shop, 1950
Frank Lloyd Wright, San Francisco, California, 1950

124

Above and preceding overleaf:
Freeman House, 1953
Frank Lloyd Wright, Los Angeles, California, 1923

Wright? My response, expressed honestly, is a simple one. There have been no "differences" in my composing a scene as long as I can objectively relate to each man's theme. My prospect of extracting plan, siting, and design elements is not an intricate one; just as long as I assemble them in an orderly, albeit appealing composition. That evolves according to my ability, my process of clearly "reading" the plan of a space and establishing an interplay between scenes. This is evident in many of my photographs. Kurt Forster, architectural historian, during a visit to my studio, observed an enlarged view of Wright's Guggenheim interior. He remarked to his associate: "Often one photograph creates a fulfilling statement. This one says it all."

Strange how lives become interwoven! In 1948, I received a call from Esther McCoy; she was entering into an expanded writing career; architectural subjects would be her bailiwick. My post-war years were saturated with assignments which could provide numerous projects for her to reveal to a wide range of publications. We embarked upon storytelling pursuits. Her skilled expressions, honed by the years of working with a number of architects, including Schindler, provided her with an objective analysis of design. Her articles were enthusiastically welcomed. By the early 1950s we were receiving assignments from a wide range of general and specialized publications. Esther was skilled in researching the work of pioneer architects: Greene and Greene, Bernard Maybeck, Bruce Goff, Henry Trost and George Wyman. They represented a formidable array in their creation of designs which made marked impressions on architects throughout the world.

Our presentations of the work of Frank Lloyd Wright, with his textile block houses in the Los Angeles area, provided information about his unique work that was seldom seen previously. Of particular impact, Wyman's Bradbury building of 1893, which she "discovered" in 1953, aroused universal attention after our initial presentation in *Arts and Architecture* magazine. Perhaps the productively cordial relationship we developed during our assignments was responsible for our success. As Esther put it in her story about my photography, in *Angeles* magazine of March, 1990: *Persistence of Vision: The Encompassing Eye of Architectural Photographer Julius Shulman,* "No other photographer had ever invited me to participate in the work." That involved "our heads together under the black cloth" as we analyzed compositions.

We spent over two weeks in Yucatan producing a story on Mayan structures for the *Los Angeles Times Home Magazine* in 1956.

Ennis House, 1951
Frank Lloyd Wright, Los Angeles, California, 1923

We had our heads together, I recall, as we evolved a scene from the top of a temple at Uxmal. I wish that our conversations could have been recorded. The highly appraised observations and world-wide publications of our works must be credited to Esther; what a remarkable companion she was for forty-one years. She died in December, 1989.

By the late 1950s, I was traveling to Mexico, Yucatan and Europe. I anticipated the need to create a scheduling method which would enable me to synchronize my dates. As one of my first experiments, *Progressive Architecture Magazine* had asked me to photograph Eero Saarinen's Stevens College Chapel in Columbia,

Missouri. Young and energetic, I produced a thorough coverage, interiors and exteriors in a day and one half. By the third morning of the trip, I arrived at my next destination, Oklahoma City. At the early hour scheduled I met Truett Coston, architect of St. Luke's Methodist Church, and was in full activity by 9:30 a.m. with the production of early morning views. By midday, a leisurely lunch, and by early evening, with the long days of June, I was well on the way towards completing the requested compositions, as well as my own. These included color as well as black and white scenes. The two projects were easily completed, no rush, with ample assistance from one of Coston's staff. I could have done another small building for the architect – we decided "next time", when I would photograph a major project, the American Airlines Operational and Maintenance Plant in Tulsa, Oklahoma.

With a good night's rest I took an early non-stop flight to Los Angeles the next morning, and was back in my studio before noon. I concluded that my "synchronization" was a complete success. On future combined assignments I continued producing with ease, as many as four projects at varied locations. Of course the clients were happy with the coordination of time and expenses. On occasion, with private planes, architects would fly me to my next destination – Nebraska, Kansas, Oklahoma, Missouri. I have photographed projects in no fewer than 44 of the United States over the course of my career.

I had met several architects in Israel. From those, I selected a body of works to demonstrate an ongoing progression of designs. Perhaps the more intriguing of my dual productions were the essays on the history and quarrying of marble. Not only was the marble utilized in domestic structures, but huge slabs were shipped to Belgium for processing for use on buildings throughout the world. Reportedly, King Solomon's Temple obtained marble from some of the same quarries which I had photographed during my assignments. Likewise, many Roman structures in Tiberius, Caesarea, Ashkelon, and many other Roman communities built so many years ago all utilized vast quantities of the marble and limestone so readily available.

One of the executives from the Lime and Stone Institute of Israel drove us through Israel visiting many of the projects which were to be photographed for the story during an extended two-week period. He was an authority on historical and biblical events, significant in the course of the assignments. He stopped his car one

Above:
The Governor's Palace at Uxmal, 1956
Yucatan, Mexico

Left:
The Pyramid of the Magician at Uxmal, 1956
Yucatan, Mexico

Solomon R. Guggenheim Museum, 1964
Frank Lloyd Wright, New York, New York, 1955–59

132

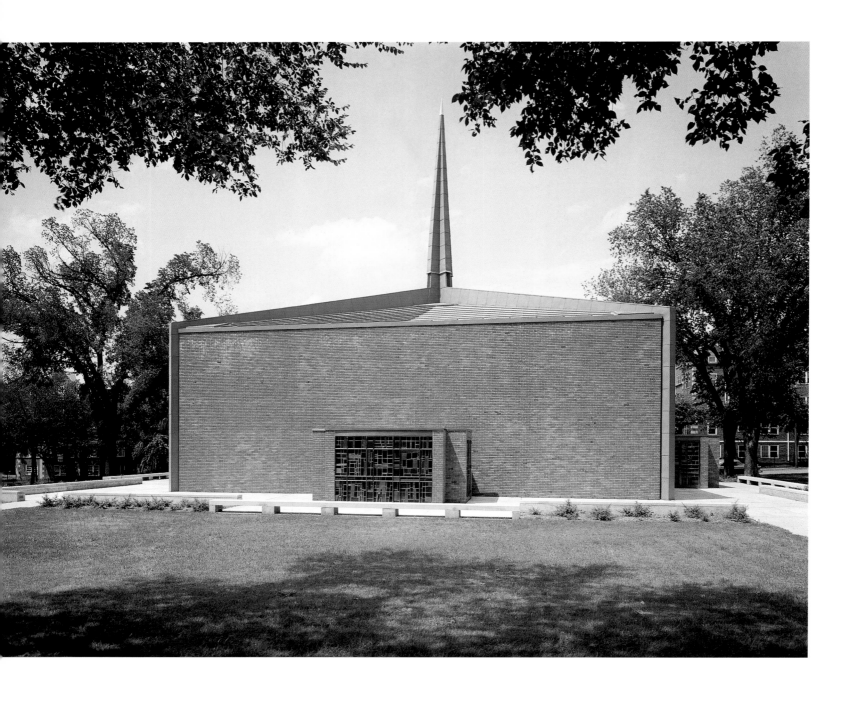

Stevens College Chapel, 1957
Eero Saarinen, Columbia, Missouri, 1955

day on a hill overlooking a valley: "Down there is the location where David confronted Goliath," he said with enthusiasm as we viewed the magnificent landscape. Another segment of my visit occurred in Ashkelon with its Roman ruins. The columns were so well preserved that one could not help but marvel at the craftsmanship of their execution.

Throughout my prolonged career I have been closely related to all facets of my productions: I have worked towards improving, within the broad scope of my photography, a wide range of

confrontations with product producers, editors, photographic organizations, publishers, journalists, and print and processing film laboratories.

I recall that, while I was photographing the Business Education Building by architect Richard Neutra and focusing my camera, a blurred object suddenly appeared on the ground glass of the camera. Lifting my head I observed Neutra holding a small branch within inches of my camera lens. "Richard," I exclaimed, "what are you doing?" He said, that he wanted to "cover the area where the building met the concrete walk, the contractor didn't do it right!" I was surprised that an architect with whom I had collaborated so closely could err in his intention. I explained that if such an exposure had been executed all we would have had on the film would be a distorted image of both the building and the leaves. I asked Neutra to look at the buildings as he viewed it through the camera. As he did, I held his branch for the intended image. "It's out of focus!" he exclaimed. An elementary lesson for a great architect: do not expect a photographer to undo a construction blunder. The photograph, taken my way, was selected for the exhibition. Neutra was honored posthumously. I am certain, those viewing that photograph were not in the least concerned with the contractor's blunder. Neither am I.

There were occasions, however, when I was at a loss when, for example, an assured landscape failed to materialize. What to do? For a national magazine, a deadline for the delivery of 8" x 10" color transparencies was the requirement. My assistant and I skillfully cut walnut tree branches (on the property) and borrowed a quantity of flowering plants in containers from a nearby nursery. With some careful arrangement, natural looking compositions were achieved. Months later, on publication, many readers inquired as to the names of the plants on various pages of the story. Suffice to say however, after publication, the happy editor scolded me when I disclosed the true story of my landscaping venture. Even though I provided accurate botanical references for identification, she was not placated. The developer of the house was pleased, although the realistic landscaping puzzled him, after admitting that he failed to adhere to his agreement with the magazine. Perhaps, he offered, "I should hire you as a landscape consultant."

In another incident, working with a staff associate of a major national magazine, we had an agreement in Southern California with a garden editor to feature a luxuriant vine, Copa de Ora, or commonly named, Cup of Gold. The assignment was not scheduled

Above:
Marble Quarry, 1959
Acre, Israel

Left:
Helzev University, 1959
Jersusalem, Israel

during the blossoming period, but the writer, familiar with a company which provided botanically authentic blossoms for motion picture studios, arranged to have a quantity delivered. They were attached to the extensive patio roof's vine expanse, and the resultant photograph was enthusiastically admired – and published. But that was not the end of this adventure. Following publication, the associate who had made the arrangement for the blossoms told the editor-in-chief at lunch, how she had acquired them, anticipating a wave of gratitude for her initiative. Instead, the associate was soundly condemned for daring to violate the high standards of the magazine. "Your procedure was not proper," she proclaimed. The associate protested. Countless numbers of motion picture viewers accepted the blossoms as authentic. That should be proof enough. The artificial flower company had on its staff a highly appraised expert whose experience vouchsafed botanical correctness. How petty on the part of the editor. And how disillusioning to us.

We all learn from those confrontations. We who are performing in the processes of faultless image building should not be put off by such behavior. As for me, I learned in another assignment. For a major national publication, I was asked to photograph a prominent landscape architect's azalea garden in full bloom, a sea of what appeared as white butterflies. We were to produce a wide-angle vista of the garden. Unfortunately the Spring season of bloom coincided with the normal coastal incursion of fog in Southern California, often lasting weeks on end. Alas, by the time the sun came out, most of the blossoms had faded away. Left alone on this particular session, my assistant and I created our own "butterflies" from a box of white Kleenex. The response from the landscape editor: "Julius, you did it again. Congratulations for the unexpected beauty!" As a result, the landscape architect received scores of letters asking: "How can we learn to achieve such a rewarding sea of white butterflies?" But I never disclosed how I mastered those natural-looking blossoms.

It would appear to me that one way to clarify critiques would be to simply visit an owner of a home or hospital, or any other structure for that matter. Once, during the photography of a new home with Richard Neutra, while he was resting, the owner and I were discussing his feelings about the house's qualities. At one period, he suddenly pointed a finger at me: "I hold you responsible! During our initial meetings, Neutra brought books and photographs, mostly taken by you. My wife and I were so taken with those beautiful expressions that we then and there signed a contract. We

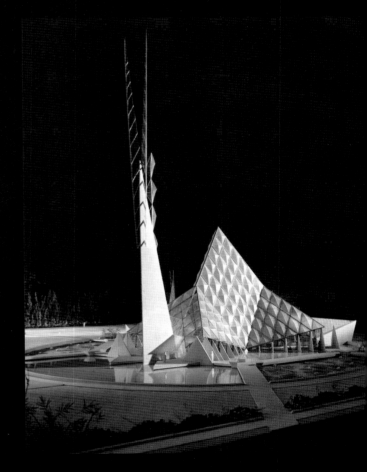

Frey House, 1953
Albert Frey, Palm Springs, California, 1947–53

Frey House II, 1964
Albert Frey, Palm Springs, California, 1963/64

accepted, in good faith, Neutra's final plan with the assumption that he had applied my wife's input, her comments on the floor plan. Neither of us could 'read' an architect's plan. In the process of construction we observed questionable areas. Neutra placated us: everything will be to your complete satisfaction."

At this point, if a critic had visited the house with Neutra, or alone, how could he have worded his comments to phrase a client's unhappiness! To the owners, the house did not represent their feelings. The kitchen and the living spaces were not placed according

wrapping paper. When the puzzled architect protested, the artist responded, "I should have given you a compass – the windowed area was to have been oriented to the north, not west!" But the publication of the house was favorably described – the editor had no occasion to be alerted to the blunder by the architect or the artist. Therefore, my protest is that reviews of designs as disclosed are not necessarily objective. I have lived with architecture, now over 62 years, far longer than most critics or writers. To me the architect is an important person whose contributions have made the world a

Right:
Palm Springs City Hall, 1968
Albert Frey, Palm Springs, California, 1952–57

Overleaf:
Loewy House, 1947
Albert Frey, Palm Springs, California, 1946/47

genuine sanctuary for multitudes. A poet phrased it beautifully: The sun beamed down its golden rays, The earth was an immense jewel! Is it not the responsibility of the critics and writers to seek in their reportage those elements of design which continue to reinforce those contributions, rather than attempting to demolish them?

Then there was the expansion of Albert Frey's original house through to completed turret structure, Rosa's book, an exhibition of his career – the latter at Santa Barbara's University of California Art Museum, followed by a showing at the Desert Museum in Palm Springs, California, and then to various exhibitions in Albert's home country, Switzerland, and in England. The work of Albert Frey has attracted international curiosity because he seldom pursued attempts at "promotion". Accordingly, his designs were acclaimed considerably among architects and architectural critics.

There was a drastic change in Frey's lifestyle at a time when he began to search for another location than the floor of the desert where he had lived for so many decades. This change in venue was prompted by the encroachment of many other houses around the perimeter of his property and he wanted more privacy. Therefore, he located a high site on the side of Mt. San Jacinto. It was one of the highest sites ever built upon in the Palm Springs area, giving him a dramatic view of the whole desert floor and also, of course, of the sprawling Palm Springs town. Here on his new site, he lived with rattlesnakes, foxes, and other denizens of the desert as well as feeding hungry quail every day. Receiving visitors from around the world, who had seen the book on Albert Frey and had witnessed the exhibits of his work, was indeed a wonderful change in Albert's lifestyle for he had always been something of a hermit, living alone and seldom visiting with people from other areas. Now, even the fashion magazines used his home as a background for style demonstrations.

What if?

Seldom in building history has there been such frenetic activity as during the 1950s. Remarkably, however, during that decade of post-war construction activity, design trends by architects were apparently quite static. With shortages of building equipment and supplies, even experienced labor was in short supply. Building costs rose astronomically. Architects restricted adventuresome design statements. But as the 1960s evolved into a more "deep-breathing" period for architects, greater flexibility in forms and materials resulted. My assignments, several of which are illustrated here, demonstrated this clearly. The variance in form identification can be readily noted in some of my projects, which ranged over widely dispersed areas of the United States: Bernard Judge's Dome, a variation of Buckminister Fuller's geodesic exercise and Thomas McNulty's free-formed concrete structure situated on the east coast in Massachusetts. Even John Lautner's richness of form evolution during more recent decades is evident in his Silvertop format of the mid-1960s.

But on the other aspect of design discipline some architects adhered to the orthodoxy of past decades. This was widely practiced by Richard Neutra. Although his designs of the 1930s, when I first photographed his Kun house, were reminiscent of the International Style, Neutra's refinement of form and material selection produced a marked departure in the 1960s, notably that his Des Moines, Iowa house. It is difficult for those of us living amidst a world of modernist architecture to grasp how unusual and extreme this house appeared to Iowans. But the owners of the house were generous in their desire to demonstrate that the "advanced" design was most suitable to Iowa's climate. Another variant, the Robert Skinner home, although considered by many as "severe" on the exterior, illustrates how architects of that period were embracing a refinement of their interiors. Architects Buff and Hensman, in their own interpretation of a continuing design practice, created a boldly executed beach house for a young family. It served beautifully for a growing, active family's lifestyle. Another example of "orthodoxy" applied to a specific program.

"Dome" House, 1962
Bernard Judge, Los Angeles, California, 1960

Overleaf:
Skinner House, 1959
Robert Skinner, Beverly Hills, California, 1955

McNulty House, 1970
Mary Otis Stevens and Thomas McNulty, Lincoln,
Massachusetts, 1965

Above and preceding overleaf:
Reiner Residence (Silvertop), 1964
John Lautner, Los Angeles, California, 1963

The meager number of commercial photographers in many areas of the country, mostly inexperienced in architects' needs, created a demand for those of us who were specializing in the subject. Personally, I was alarmed. The economic growth of my area, Southern California, was more dynamic than most other parts of the country. The demand for my services necessitated longer-ranged scheduling for my out-of-state requests. To alleviate the situation, I had structured seminars and workshops with A.I.A. chapters and schools of architecture to demonstrate techniques of design photography. We invited area commercial photographers to participate. For students and working architects we encouraged improvement of their own camera use by teaming up with photographers. The latter was one of my earliest processes – the close

liaison thus enabled us to coordinate definite statements useful for publications. The next step, in the 1960s, was my decision to produce a book on the subject. My first publication, with the Whitney Library of Design, *Photographing Architecture and Interiors*, was an immediate success. It was followed, in 1974, by another volume: *The Photography of Architecture and Design*. That went into three printings! Both books circulated internationally, as instruments of instruction for architects, students, and photographers. A rewarding by-product, the illustrations which I had selected were of qualitative designs. Soon I was receiving requests from writers and publishers to acquire many of them for books on the subject. I would be happy to learn that my efforts were instrumental in furthering the expertise of photographers.

Above and overleaf:
Malin Residence (Chemosphere), 1960
John Lautner, Hollywood, California, 1960

Culver City Auditorium, 1963
Flewelling and Moody, Culver City, California, 1963

160

A major project in my life was the Architectural Panel project "Environment USA". It involved attending, in 1962–63, meetings of a dynamic and daring organization of young designers, including artists involved in creative disciplines, and foremost a body of working and constructive architects motivated by their conviction that our environment was suffering in its ever-increasing demise, the apparent lack of concern by the public. I volunteered to explore environmental pluses executed by leading architects throughout the United States. After almost a year and a half of photography, we assembled an exhibition of over 150 30" x 40" enlargements. The members of the Architectural Panel in conjunction with the representatives of the California Museum of Science and Industry structured a display which opened in July, 1964. Following the above

Preceding overleaf:
Architectural Panel Project: Environment USA,
View of Centennial City, 1964

Left:
Rancho California, 1964
Temecula, California

Right:
St. Peter's Church, 1964
Mario Ciampi, Pacifica, California

Channel Heights Housing Project, 1948
Richard Neutra, San Pedro, California, 1942

Geriatrics Hospital, 1962
Ramberg and Lowrey, Dana Point, California, 1962

exhibition, numbers of museums, galleries, and environmental organizations throughout the country requested similar exhibitions. During the National AIA convention in 1964, in Washington D.C., a representative section of the exhibition was presented. The *AIA Journal* published a piece on the exhibit, using my Tree House photograph as the cover.

The request from the Conservancy Committee served as another testing ground for a search into my archives of "abandoned" photography. Seeking available projects, we extracted from my card file locations and other identifying facts. The project numbers led us to the appropriate prints on file, facilitating the decisions for choice of the planned tours' subjects. Attendant to the above exhibitions, which extended over a period of ten years, I presented lectures pertinent to environmental crises nationwide, and also conducted photographic workshops for architects and photographers.

Apparently the impact of all of the above aroused the interest of architects, for I received requests to perform a number of assignments wherever I travelled. Coincidental activity included meetings at architectural schools at universities – conversations with students were productive in enlightening them as to the techniques of utilizing photography as a learning tool.

Additional Midwestern assignments during ensuing years also were indicative of the advantages of carefully organized scheduling. For example, in November of 1964, I photographed for architects Crites and McConnell, Ray Crites' own house in Cedar Rapids, Iowa, Herb Greene's Cunningham residence in Oklahoma City also in November, 1964, and Coston, Frankfurt, and Short's Doctors' Building in Oklahoma City. The above scheduling not only cut travel expenses but also rationalized my laboratory processing. In this instance, with three major projects, laboratory time was allotted in advance of my return.

I had never wanted to stay away from home too long because of the ongoing demand for assignments from architects within my immediate area. It simply reflects a manner of creating quality photography without the usual pressures of running back and forth across the country for one assignment at a time.

Given the architectural and photographic wealth of the assignments, some of my work also involved rigorous security checks. Late in 1966, while photographing a project, TRW, for architects A.C. Martin Associates, an encounter served to illustrate the rigidity of security. In my overall scene of the project, a security guard can be

Above:
Tree House, 1964
Architect unknown

Left:
Rosen House, 1964
Craig Ellwood Associates, Brentwood, California, 1962

167

Crites Residence, 1964
Crites and McConnell, Cedar Rapids, Iowa, 1963

Cunningham Residence, 1964
Herb Greene, Oklahoma City, Oklahoma, 1964

seen at the left side of the view approaching on his cycle. Satisfied with my identification, he suggested that in Russia at that time of international insecurity, I would have been surrounded by a swarm of armed guards. In retrospect the incident seemed humorous; after all, with my large tripod-mounted camera, I was clearly violating the company's "no photography" edicts.

The interior areas of the plant, accessible with security clearance, were composed as structural and production scenes. Even with highly disciplined scrutiny in my original access provisions, I chuckled, amused as my accompanying guard requested a look through my 4" x 5" camera ground glass as I prepared a view. "It's upside down," he exclaimed, apparently never having experienced such a viewing. No problem with the view's breach of security, for what the white-garbed workers were producing was not in the least discernible. Scenes were valuable to the architects in their rendering of interrelated compositions of major experimental and production areas.

Because of total security of interior spaces, other projects were photographed for the value of their architectural exteriors alone. I was permitted to photograph the reception area of architect Charles Luckman's Nortronics project. The interior view had to rely upon late afternoon sunlight; none of my light equipment was allowed. But as a hint to photographers: could artificial lighting produce a better effect? I took another scene using infrared-film. That composition created quite a stir when I showed it to architect Luckman. "Let me show this to my staff," as he summoned them. The impact was even greater when the scene with normal film was observed. I only wished that more photographers availed themselves of the opportunities in infrared's capacity of enhancing visual expressions.

In 1958 I photographed Convair Astronautics in San Diego, California for the architects Pereira and Luckman. The production of Atlas intercontinental missiles was involved. To me, although it was a rewarding assignment, this project disturbed me. If only the billions of dollars spent on weapons of destruction could be detoured towards a peaceful use of the funds. Photographically this assignment afforded me an opportunity to exercise my skills; there were numerous choices of compositions. The cloud-filled skies, in particular, so responsive to my filtering, helped to delineate and fortify the structural graphics.

As an adjunct to my industrial subjects, I selected key "boiler room" illustrations. All buildings of widely differing functions

TRW plant, 1966
*A.C. Martin Associates, Redondo Beach, California,
1966*

Northrop Corporation, Nortronics Division, 1961
Charles Luckman and Associates, Palos Verdes,
California, 1961

require a complexity of operational facilities: power sources, heating, air-conditioning, water supplies and distribution and many other needs. I realize that architects, engineers and photographers seldom pay heed to disclosing the significance of those operational necessities. During my assignments I have emphasized this with dramatic views, much to the surprise of many clients who had not anticipated that such a "mundane" subject could add to a neglected dimension of their designs.

The Bethlehem Steel Co. project in November, 1961, entailed my spending considerable time being flown around in their company plane to various eastern colleges, mostly Ivy League schools, to illustrate the revision and reconstruction of many of the eastern colleges. Bethlehem Steel Co. was the sponsor organization for Lehigh University in Bethlehem, Pennsylvania, and they were going to finance the construction of new buildings. The photographs I took on this extended trip throughout the East Coast were used for study purposes by the company's architects.

Convair Astronautics, 1958
Pereira and Luckman, San Diego, California, 1958

I was called by the Bethlehem Steel Company's President, Frank Rabold, in Bethlehem, Pennsylvania, in 1961. He had become familiar with my photography in his research among publishers and architects. Met at Kennedy Airport, early after a night flight, I was driven to Bethlehem. The American Airline president, a friend and business associate of Mr. Rabold, had arranged for Bethlehem's limousine to drive onto the field to unload my cases of equipment from the plane. This gentleman had known of my photography of American's Operational and Maintenance facilities in Tulsa, Oklahoma a few years previously. Ushered into the Bethlehem office compound to meet heads of various departments, the morning was devoted to coordinating the planned assignments: the Chief Executive Officer was retiring. A bound book of the photographs of Bethlehem's holdings on the east coast was to be presented to him at a farewell banquet. The initial project entailed the photography of Bethlehem's huge new research structure. That was followed by a drive into the Pocono Mountain area where Bethlehem had estab-

175

Bethlehem Steel Co. Houses, 1961
Bethlehem, Pennsylvania

lished a vast recreation area for executives, heads of departments and visiting dignitaries. For two days I wandered around the various spaces, photographing beautifully maintained riding horse and farm equipment stables – it was a working farm as well. Additionally I photographed a compound of individual guest residences.

My next visit was to the Bethlehem Steamship Company offices in Manhattan. A few general views had been requested. That facility required none of my lighting equipment, the internal illumination was so thorough. Then I was driven to La Guardia airfield to board Bethlehem's company plane to be flown to what was the highlight of my assignment series: Bethlehem was the location of Lehigh University; the Steel Company was the sponsor of the institution and was proceeding, with my photography, to structure a program for a vast project to rehabilitate the campus buildings and a redevelopment of "downtown."

The core of Bethlehem's study: Lehigh was an old-time institution, considered with a group of other aged learning centers, as Ivy League colleges. Most of those old-time buildings were covered with overgrown cloaks of ivy. I was to be flown to each of the campuses to photograph the new post-war buildings for a demonstration of design directions of the architecture. The process of thus maintaining a physical uniformity of the colleges' appearances would be further validated by the campuses' nostalgic visual aspects. Most of the institutions were entered through grand gateways reminiscent of old English estates. These added colorful accents to my detailing. The group included Harvard, Yale, Cornell, Wellesley, Dartmouth, and of course Lehigh.

The logistics of what appeared a complex procedure were organized. I was driven from my hotel in Bethlehem early each morning to the airport, where the pilot and co-pilot, with a pre-

Ezra Stiles and Morse Colleges,
Yale University, 1961
Eero Saarinen, New Haven, Connecticut,
1958–62

Yale University David S. Ingalls Hockey Rink,
1961
Eero Saarinen, New Haven, Connecticut,
1953–59

Chapel of the Massachusetts Institute of
Technology, 1961
Eero Saarinen, Cambridge, Massachusetts,
1953–55

determined flight schedule, would have the twin-engine Aero-Commander plane ready for take-off. At our destination, a waiting car would drive to the campus, where a "guide" would conduct a tour. Newer structures would be photographed with older traditional ones to illustrate the essence of the Ivy League appearance. With my equipment stored in the plane during the group of assignments, I operated swiftly.

All the planned assignments took two weeks. Every moment was comfortably and smoothly paced; there were no complications. The final day's goodbye came with a casual request from the company's treasurer: "Don't forget, send us a bill!" I did just that when sending the completed photographs. It entered my mind at the moment of leaving, no one had ever asked how much the complex assignments would cost. That has been a recurring feature of numerous assignments throughout my career. I attribute it to my constant performance. Never have I required a "redo." What I charge per day or a flat fee for composite assignments as the Bethlehem survey is considered as favorable; all founded upon a know-how fueled by one hundred per cent efficient utilization of time and facilities.

Another form of composite assignments could apply to two rewarding requests. On the completion of their North American headquarter complex in Torrance, the Toyota company executives inquired of the architects, Pereira and Luckman, as to the best photographer to produce a total image of the project for a report to headquarters in Tokyo. I was recommended, but how gratifying, to find that Tokyo in the meantime, exploring the realm of United States' photographers, had also concluded that I was the one! With two assistants, I spent twelve days on the most intricate assignment in all my years. Every aspect of the company's operation was explored with their officials. After all they opined, "We are the largest importer of Japanese automobiles to the United States. This is the key to our operations. A complete indexing of the functions here will be analyzed – computerized from your photographs."

To produce consistency in my photographs was not a problem. I had complete cooperation from the many departments of the complex. Each composition represented associated functions. Each evening one of my associates returned to the studio for the processing. Our color laboratory arranged for an evening pick-up

Toyota Plant, 1983
Pereira and Luckman, Torrance, California, 1983

and processing, delivering the color transparencies of the day's exposures to the complex the next mid-morning. We all gathered around for an examination – officials and my assistants, for a few moments of inspection. No failures; after the coffee break, on to the next elements – twelve days of 100% production!

As if the Toyota projection of success required an encore, within a short period of time, another request came, this time for the Nissan Company, Toyota's competitor in numbers of imports to the United States. They had built their American design headquarters in La Jolla, California. All Nissan cars for American distribution were designed in that facility. The Nissan assignment, although not as intricate as Toyota's, was an enjoyable one. The design and ex-perimental spaces, together with the innovative public and exterior areas, presented problem-free compositions. It gave me great personal satisfaction to be selected by the two largest Japanese car manufacturers. The assignments, near the end of my active career, added fuel to my reservoir of self-esteem. How rewarding to arrive at such an elevated role in my profession, especially within the framework of completely successful clients' relations.

In December 1959, I photographed the restored sod-roofed cluster of ancient houses in Rauland, Norway, for the *New York Times*. This project features my use of a Superwide Hasselblad camera and a small kit of lighting equipment. This was especially important because the house was like a miniature doll house and there would not have been much room to work with a large camera so I was fortunate in having selected the small equipment.

The above assignment for the *New York Times* magazine originated at one of the *Times* editors' office in New York. We were discussing my forthcoming Scandinavian trip in 1959. "Yes, we will be travelling through the southwestern Norway area." Yes, I knew where the town of Rauland was situated. I would be happy to photograph interiors of one of the houses, plus general exteriors. So there I was, a drenching rainstorm forcing us to enjoy two days of relaxing dining and rest. By the third day I was able to take exteriors from under a large umbrella (provided by the Hotel Rauland management). For interiors, my wide-angle Hasselblad was perfectly suited to cover the tiny rooms. My lighting equipment consisted of small reflectors using the smallest flashbulbs available. The Gods of photography were faithful to me. As with every assignment I per-formed throughout the world, every exposure turned out perfectly (to the delight of all concerned). I have persistently pleaded with

Kahala Hilton Hotel, 1964
Killingsworth, Brady and Associates, Honolulu, Hawaii, 1964

photographers: discipline yourselves, stop depending upon instruments or meters to do your thinking!

An incident which could have generated a drastic repercussion in my life occurred in New York during one of my editorial visits in 1961. I was in the office of a friend, John Maximus, an editorial consultant, graphic designer and publication authority. He had been commissioned to revise the entire production of Radio Corporation of America's (RCA) house organ, *Electronic Age*. Maximus, familiar with my photographic collaboration with the architectural press of the world, much of it in New York, suggested that I share space in his office to install a broad segment of my photography to facilitate access by the many writers and publishers to whom I had provided photographs since the onset of my career. Maximus' office, in the RCA Building of Rockefeller Center, was located within walking distance of many of the organizations I served in Manhattan. He would arrange for his secretary to process appointments, organize the demonstrations of the photographic material and coordinate with me the availability of selected projects.

The potential of such representation seemed to offer an ideal means of exposing my current as well as archival photography directly to publications. During the ensuing discussions with editorial colleagues, the likelihood of my establishing a "branch" in New York was discussed. Enthusiastically and unanimously, the consensus was: "We would be keeping you busy doing assignments during your east coast visit!" Apparently, although anticipating ready access to my files, the editors, as Maximus interpreted, were "anxious to acquire more of Shulman's touch in their publications." How fateful their declarations, for I was immediately faced with a big decision.

I decided that there would be no running back and forth between both coasts of the United States. At the time I was working to full capacity, so great were the numbers of assignments. Becoming a transcontinental commuter was not to be a favored "occupation". If I had succumbed to the temptation of accepting Maximus' invitation and assignments from editors on the east coast the physical drain on my well-being would have been detrimental. My pace of work in Los Angeles, with my home and studio in a densely-wooded environment, was measured and determined without pressures of deadlines. I was not about to hire additional assistants as some suggested. When inquiries for assignments were presented, I was to do the work; my "expertise" was the point of the request.

If the New York proposal had become a reality, I would most likely have constructed another episode to add to my essay on that subject. I tried to visualize, even remotely, what my life would offer: how could I have maintained my free and happy existence without burning my candle at both ends? Now at age 88, pursuing associations with publishers and writers in the production of books and magazine articles throughout the world, I can still look forward to my 68th year of skiing this coming winter.

Researching a storage room in my studio, long neglected, I came upon a surprising number of photographs which had been withdrawn from files in order to create space for the then current assignments. Now, after a time span of more than a decade, came the realization that the designs represented by the photographs were of a quality often equal to or even surpassing those of current practice. Among the projects, I uncovered two sets of photographs by an architect, Raul Garduno. I had received the assignments from editors of the *Los Angeles Times Home Magazine*. For many years there appeared, widely read every Sunday, brilliantly illustrated dissertations on the designs of the most creative architects in Southern

California. The two houses illustrated herein are indicative of those. The photographs provide examples of residential architecture prevalent in the 1960s era when they were taken. As in many of my searches to locate long "abandoned" architects, I was delighted to discover that Garduno was still alive and active. His designs are engaged in Mexico, at the tip of Baja California, in Cabo San Lucas. I was pleased to learn of Garduno's whereabouts for his presence revived my spirits. We had not seen each other for over 30 years. I have in my studio enlarged prints of some of his work and it is gratifying to observe how positively and favorably visiting architects consider his designs.

In 1964, on the ski slopes of Mammoth Mountain, I heard my name called on the loud speakers. At the office I was informed of the message. I called interior designer, William Pahlman in New York. "How would you like to do a project for me in Hong Kong?" It involved the thorough photographing of a new hotel in the Kowloon

area. I quickly packed my equipment and left for home. Within 48 hours I was in flight. With associations in many parts of the world I had placed calls prior to departure. One provided me with an assignment for another designer in Kowloon. I would produce an essay on his new home.

On the slopes of Kowloon Peak, I found a palette of colourful scenes to assemble for my camera's viewing. I was house guest for nine days. My host had called an architect friend who asked if I would do his new home, also in Kowloon. His wife was the interior designer. So, armed with three assignments, I was prepared to devote myself to a new adventure; I had never been to Hong Kong. I stayed in Hong Kong-Kowloon for nineteen excitingly productive days. But the beginning was a challenge. When I arrived I learned that the

Hotel, 1964
William Pahlman, Hong Kong, 1963

Overleaf:
Godfrey Residence, 1964
Gerald Godfrey, Hong Kong

power in Hong Kong was provided by a 220 volt line, whereas my equipment was all made for 110 volts as we have in the United States. It was not easy to convert the 220 volt source of power down to 110 volts to provide for my eight lights which I had brought with me. We achieved with four 220 volt plugs a means of dividing the voltage into two for each pair of lights. Hotel management assigned a group of youngsters no more than 14 years of age to assist me while I was working on the overall coverage of the hotel. They seem to understand. Two of them ran off to an electrical supply company, returned with the above-mentioned plugs, and my nine days of photography with the brilliant assistance of this team of youngsters went off smoothly. Every picture turned out perfectly. I was also able to ship my exposed film through the architects' courier service to the

United States, and receive, as they were processed, a coded statement by cable that they were all turning out perfectly, color and black and white.

I photographed the house of Gerald Godfrey, an interior designer who worked with a major interior firm in Kowloon, and I was his house guest for several days during the total of 19 days that I stayed in the Hong Kong-Kowloon area. I attended a Hong Kong theater with the Kinoshitas and we saw the film of Elizabeth Taylor as Cleopatra. In this film her voice was dubbed, speaking Chinese, and it was a beautiful experience to know what she was saying and yet not able to understand Chinese.

In June, 1965, I photographed the Cathedral of the Risen Christ in Omaha, Nebraska, by Leo Daly Co. The exterior photograph of the structure was taken from the inside of a jeep. The parking lot actually became a shallow lake and the church was reflected entirely in this body of water. A 16" x 20" print was made of this at the request of the architects and it was sent to the Pope in the Vatican City. He was amazed, in his letter to the architects, at the beauty of the scene and was curious to know more about how the picture was taken.

Photographing architect Richard Neutra's Maslon residence in Cathedral City, California was a unique event in my life, and an experience which compounded itself into a most rewarding sequence. I had first photographed the house for Neutra. As was his practice, he, with two associates, removed most of what he considered undesirable furniture. Neutra was concerned with the design statements of his architectural elements. He preferred to have the photographs published in European books which favored the stark drama of his work. However, the furnishings of the Maslons were attractive and of considerable comfort. I was disturbed by Neutra's blatant disregard for the personal aspect of the interiors and arranged with Mrs Maslon to return at a favorable time to take new photographs illustrating her lifestyle. This was achieved. The resultant scenes, coupled with the renowned Maslon collection of contemporary art masterpieces (paintings and sculptures), illustrated how the Maslon lifestyle was enhanced further by the park-like environment of the richly landscaped golf course viewed through the glass walls of the house.

A request from *Connaissance Des Arts*, a prominent French art publication came just two weeks after my completion of the new Maslon photographs. They were planning a story on homes of varied

Cathedral of the Risen Christ, 1965
Leo Daly Co., Omaha, Nebraska, 1965

architectural styles in which contemporary art played a significant role. "Do you have such a home in your collection of modern homes?" I immediately assembled a package of color transparencies and black and white prints. To my amazement, after a few months, there arrived a package containing the current issue of the publication (March, 1966): a cover scene and seven pages of color photographs. Apparently the editors were so delighted with my presentation that they decided "to surprise me" with the above.

How curious too, that an architect of such great international stature was actually short-sighted about the overall design potential of his own architecture. Neutra apparently suffered no concern for demonstrating his capabilities to a broad cross section of potential clients, or exploring the opportunity to perform a bit of missionary education of a public with little or no genuine grasp of the broad potentials of great architecture. I have asked constantly, "Wasn't modern architecture compromised by such lack of communication?"

194

Another "what if"-experience with Richard Neutra in 1947, I have already described: how dangerously close I came to not photographing the world famous Kaufmann house scene. A classic example is that of architect Herb Greene's home outside of Norman, Oklahoma.

At the time, in 1963, he was an associate professor of architecture at the University of Oklahoma. I was photographing the Bavinger house by architect Bruce Goff, also at the University of Oklahoma architectural school, for *Horizon*, an art oriented publication of a book pursuing a story about Bavinger, head of the art department at the University. During the progression of the house photography, with the assistance of an architectural student, he asked if I would like to see the nearby Greene house. As usual, with ample time (I never crowded my life even at that period), I accepted the invitation by the Greenes to visit that evening. I had completed my *Horizon* assignment. After the student had expressed his thoughts about the house, I anticipated a relaxing, exploratory evening. That was in October, 1963. The Greene house was indeed all the student

Maslon House, photographed with (bottom left) and without (bottom right) Richard Neutra, 1963
Richard Neutra, Cathedral City, California, 1962

Bavinger House, 1963
Bruce Goff, Norman, Oklahoma, 1950–55

Preceding overleaf and above:
Greene House ("Prairie Chicken"), 1963
Herb Greene, Norman, Oklahoma, 1962

Overleaf:
United Covenant Presbyterian Church, 1967
Crites and McConnell, Danville, Illinois, 1967

had suggested. When we arrived, there were several members of the University of Oklahoma School of Architecture faculty and a few graduate school students. I was remembered as having been at the campus in 1950, photographing Goff's classical Chapel model. I was enthusiastic in my admiration of the house and suggested that I felt its significance as a milestone.

The world of 1963 had generated a freedom among the liberally active younger generations throughout the country. The Greene house design exhibited a broad essence of that freedom. "I have a few days to spare," I told the Greenes, "and would appreciate your allowing me to photograph it so I could show the photographs to editor friends in New York; the following week would be ideal."

As occurs so frequently, architects' own homes are seldom "completed." So with Herb Greene: "I still have several incomplete details." His wife, a beautiful redhead, grasping the rare opportunity for publication: "Herb, you know that it will take considerable time

to complete your proposed unfinished details." Turning to me, she
suggested that they would put me up for the duration of my visit!
But Herb was dubious. What if I had not been persistent and bowed
out, agreeing to wait until next year? That "what if" would have
resulted in an editorial publicity tragedy related as follows: Others
among the visitors, especially his colleagues, joined in: "Herb, this is
your first house – what an opportunity to have it photographed by a
man of Shulman's stature, delivering the photographs a week later to
top publications in New York." He agreed. With enthusiastic
applause from all around, we joined in a joyous toast to the project. I
moved in with all my photographic gear and my personal bags and
worked for four days. A week later in New York, with processed
color transparencies in hand (these were processed by an
acquaintance with a lab), I called my friend, Mary Hamman,
Modern Living editor at *Life* magazine: "Mary, I have something to
show you." Trusting my enthusiasm she invited me to lunch "as fast

Getty Estate, 1965
Sutton Place, Surrey, England

as you can get off your seat." We placed the six transparencies (all the
color I had taken with my 4" x 5" camera) on her viewing table.
Without a response she reached for her telephone, addressed *Life*
editor, George Thompson: "Get down here as quickly as you can."
Within moments he appeared, viewed the films, turned to Mary:
"When can we publish them?" The rest is history. A month later
(November, 1963) a brilliant spread was published. Herb Greene
became a hero. A position with the University of Delaware School of
Architecture was offered to him. A few years later he moved to Penn
State University. *Progressive Architecture* magazine had also published
the house. It was followed with a cover and full presentation of
another new house by Greene in Oklahoma City. European editors
of prominent magazines also published his work.

Perhaps I should add one more story to the above experience. It
resulted in architect Ray Crites, and his firm, Crites & McConnell of

Cedar Rapids, Iowa, earning a national AIA award for the firm's United Covenant Presbyterian Church in Danville, Illinois, 1967. On approaching Danville in our chartered plane flying from Cedar Rapids, the control tower, advised of our arrival to do photographs, suggested that weather was murky and that it would not be a good day for photography. "What if?"

When asked by Crites whether we should turn back, I responded that I felt that as long as we were approaching Danville, we should circle the church site at least one time to see for ourselves. After the circle flight I requested that we land and go to work. With infrared film I cut through the murk – we certainly did not require a "picture postcard" sky for my kind of photography. Suffice to say that we spent the day on interior and exterior scenes. Crites and McConnell later that year entered the project in the National AIA program and received an esteemed Honor citation.

In 1965, there was a rewarding change in pace from the usual architectural assignments. The president of a neighboring bank, Bart Lytton, had acquired one of Henry Moore's sculptures while on a trip to London. Announcing its installation on the grounds of the bank, Mr. Lytton in full page newspaper advertisements offered, for the best photographs of the sculpture, a trip to England to meet Henry Moore and to photograph more of his sculptures at his studios. At the same time Mr. Lytton had arranged for an interview with oil magnate J. Paul Getty at his mansion in Surrey, south of London. While visiting Mr. Getty, the opportunity presented itself to photograph the centuries old estate.

The competition was open to amateurs and professionals, indeed a tempting invitation to participate. Only a short distance from my home/studio in the Hollywood Hills, I visited the gardens of the bank early one Sunday morning. The bold forms of the sculpture were enhanced by the revealing early morning light. Moore's details were brilliantly exposed. Rather than set up my 4" x 5" view camera, I felt that my Hasselblad with its choice of lenses would be suitable for the exercise. The resulting black and white and color photographs apparently impressed the jury, composed of prominent artists and art historians. They unanimously presented me with the "prize" trip. I was to visit the sculptor, Henry Moore, in his studio on six acres of garden and studios at Much Haddam, north of London. He was renowned for his creative expressions emanating from interpretations of natural forms. My assignment was to produce an essay on a wide variety of his sculptural forms. The

Bart Lytton and J. Paul Getty in Getty's estate in Sutton Place, 1965

visit, however, was not a cordial one. From the onset I sensed friction. He was impersonal in his attitude towards me – perhaps prompted by his not agreeing with my compositions of his works at his studios.

Perhaps Moore in his observation of my viewing of his work either suspected or realized that I was "all business". In the process of touring the estate and its six studios I had not queried him as to evolution of design or form. Perhaps since his work was internationally published, with many photographers and writers in the environs, he had anticipated that I would be plying him with questions, docile and humble in the presence of the great Moore! During the positioning of my tripod-mounted 4 x 5 inch view camera for a study of Moore's *Reclining Figure – Exterior Form* I observed Moore standing at a position removed from my selected composition. He carried a Rolliflex camera, eyeing the sculpture. He

Reclining Figure – Exterior Form, 1965
Henry Moore, 1953/54

called to me: "Shulman, yours is not the correct point of view for this piece." I did not move my camera. Instead, pointing to the figure, I indicated how and why I had chosen that position as the forms responded to sunlight and shadow. I had selected the most opportune moment of light. "I am viewing the structure and form as I would in respecting an architectural form's statement." Moore responded by walking away; or did he sulk? But back home, my photographs were highly praised by art critics.

During an overflowing audience lecture and exhibition of my photographs after our return from London at the bank's auditorium, I had the appropriate opportunity to suggest to the assembled artists, photographers and art critics that even though Moore was a world-

Three Part Reclining Figure, 1965
Henry Moore, 1965

wide renowned sculptor, this did not require an acquiescence on my part to his personal viewing of his designs. I surveyed his work as I would a good architectural design: establishing a relationship of forms, colors, and presentation of materials. He did not choose to talk about what he thought of the composition of my photographs.

In an article in *Arts and Architecture* magazine, January, 1965, art critic Rosalind Wholden described what she called my "ability to reveal aspects of Moore's work rarely captured on film." She wrote: "Shulman's superb photo of the *Reclining Figure – Exterior Form*, by avoiding the usual parallel-to-the-picture-plane-view of a horizontal sculpture, an experience of the tunneling, recoiling and shrouded feeling Moore has explored in countless serpentine excavations of the body … the photographer … captures the surprising might of Moore's shapes; he encourages the timid onlooker to get close to the sculpture."

Henry Seldis, art critic of the *Los Angeles Times,* revealed his enthusiasm for my Moore photography upon viewing the prints. Editing a new book on Moore's work, Seldis informed the artist that he considered the photographs among "the best he had ever seen" of Moore's sculpture, and that he would prefer to use a number of them. He was refused: "Every image of my forms must be those wherein I attended the photography." That edict applied to another of my compositions: *Two-Piece Knife Edge.* It was perhaps the first brass effort on the part of Moore. Seldis was exalted on viewing the print. I was proud of it for my lighting of the brass surfaces produced a glowing effect; the forms of the two pieces were delineated. The rendition of the forms would not have been recorded had I not insisted on moving the sculpture off of a high pedestal to a lower one, thereby producing my effect. It was indeed ironic that the artist had elevated it so high that even without a camera, just a visual viewing of it would not have produced a favorable image. Seldis agreed, for he had seen it during a visit to Moore. He commented, "This is an ideal demonstration of how two artists, assumedly objective, should have been able to communicate." Humorously, Seldis murmured, as if Moore was near us, "It took much courage on your part to stand up to such a famous artist!" My response: "I'm famous too!" – and objective and honest.

In 1967 I undertook an extended trip throughout Uruguay as part of a specific assignment for a group of architects who wanted their work publicized in European magazines and felt that I would be the most appropriate person to take the photographs. I had been

Henry Moore, 1965

invited to produce a representative photographic essay on their work as selected by the members of the Society. To save expenses, I accepted the suggestion of the Society, that they would supply adequate assistance, so that I would not need to bring an assistant. For interiors I brought a case of lighting equipment as I did with my Hong Kong-Kowloon assignments. I was flying in the days before non-stop flights to the most distant of locations; Los Angeles with a short stay in Panama, then a night flight to Buenos Aires. High over the vast basin of the Amazon, at 37,000 feet, from the darkness below, sheets of lightning from storms over the jungles added mystery to the scene. How isolated we were in space; but the early morning arrival in Montevideo contrasted with the long night's flight, and the loneliness of the distant Amazon jungles.

State Capitol Bank, 1963
Roloff, Bailey, Bozalis, Dickinson Architects,
Oklahoma City, Oklahoma, 1963

Facal Residence, 1967
Julio Villar Marcos, Punta del Este, Uruguay

At the home of architect Julio Villar Marcos, who had coordinated the entire project, I was soon photographing the pre-scheduled structures, each with the architect represented. What a kaleidoscopic sequence of subjects appeared before my camera lenses: homes, churches, banks, shops, apartment buildings, a seminary, even thatched-roofed houses under construction. But aside from the varied styles, a highlight of the month was the gracious hospitality of everyone I met at the home of architect Miguel Amado. We lunched with his entire family – a huge bowl of spaghetti and meatballs, the centerpiece of a table laden with salads, fruits, and an assortment of drinks. On another occasion we had lunch in the Greek town of

Peropolis, founded by settlers from Greece generations ago and retaining the culinary customs of the old country. The owner of a building designed by architect Pintos Risso invited us to a sumptuous dinner at his appartment. Our host was the country's major manufacturer of fabrics. He and his wife engaged in a lively conversation while their beautiful, articulate 18 year old daughter, fresh from university in Paris, served as our hostess – elegance exemplified. From her father we learned of the problems confronting the companies which created the largest contributions to the economy. Government edicts commanded that more exports were required to offset the poor balance of trade. But ironically those very

Beach House, 1967
Gomez Platera and Lopez Rey, Punta del Este, Uruguay, 1967

215

Banco Popular del Uruguay, 1967
Eladio Destag, Montevideo, Uruguay, ca. 1965

same revenues, a great volume produced by our host's company, were so heavily taxed that he protested to his friend, Uruguay's president: "Such a form of taxation is so bureaucratic that I may as well close my business, and move to Southern France to avoid the penalty of being a good citizen!" His protest, he explained, had been taken seriously. With the abundant funds thus regained he built the apartment edifice which we had photographed. I use this example to demonstrate that what has made me a citizen of the world is my involvement in matters which ultimately affect all of us.

Further assignments took me to the region of the country's border with neighboring Argentina, the community of Punta del

Catholic Church, 1967
Eladio Destag, Atlantida, Uruguay, ca. 1965

Este. It is situated along the La Plata, the vast body of water which is actually formed by the Parana River as it disgorges endless miles of silt-laden waters into the Atlantic Ocean. One of the houses I photographed was situated on the shores of La Plata: La Caldera, so named for a vessel sunk in a storm many decades ago. Subject to height variations of tides or storms, some of its boilers become exposed: hence, the naming of the owner's home, La Caldera (boilers).

Photographing in the southern hemisphere means getting used to very different lighting conditions – every exterior exposure requires an "upside-down" visualization of a scene so as to capture maximum values of textures of a surface. I had that experience in

217

Left and right:
Banco Popular del Uruguay, 1967
Eladio Destag, Montevideo, Uruguay, ca. 1965

Overleaf:
San Carlos de Bariloche, 1967

Mexico City, when, after a view of a building that had no sun on its surface, I realized that the sun did not touch south facing surfaces, especially in the summer time.

"A la izquierda, por favor Señor," I exclaimed when, at the moment of exposure of a scene, the gardener appeared from the side of the house. The home-owner and the architect were surprised that my "Yankee" Spanish was understood; for the gardener bolted back around the corner. It is rewarding, even if one learns only basic phrases, to find that some communication is possible – anywhere in the world.

During my Uruguay project, I was introduced one evening in Montevideo to one of the architects of the newly built Bank of London in Buenos Aires. He asked if I would be visiting there, and, if so, whether I would care to photograph his firm's most significant project. What a rewarding opportunity to photograph such an innovatively designed structure; seven years in the design and construction processes. It was another highlight of my South American trip.

My flexible calendar, open ended, permitted me to spend a week in Buenos Aires – I had previously, in New York, at the *Holiday Magazine* office of the picture editor, received an assignment for Pan American Airlines to photograph for a month's illustration in the following year's calendar. The subject was the Lake district in the southwestern extremity of Argentina at the eastern base of the towering Andes. Pan American preferred a view of the major lake in the area, over 60 miles long. I delivered, not only a selection of color transparencies, but also a group of 11" x 14" black and white prints – they were made from infrared negatives which by the nature of the film penetrated all atmospheric conditions, revealing the Andes ranges at the far end of the lake. Not only did the Uruguay Society acquire a broad statement of its designs vernacular, but I introduced

much of the substance of my photography to publishers. To most, Uruguay was unknown.

While in Dubuque, Iowa, photographing a school for architects Crites and McConnell, I learned of a situation that threatened the citizens of Dubuque. Apparently a developer had proposed to the people of the city that they approve, in a forthcoming election, the annexation of an area outside the city limits. The developer owned a large parcel of land at the far end of the proposed city's expansion. The goal was to build a major shopping area, with a prime tenant, one of the nation's largest "all purpose" stores. In addition, land would be donated for new schools for the children living in the developer's new tract houses; which he would build if the ballot was favorable.

My involvement in all the above? An acquaintance in Dubuque informed me of the forthcoming vote for the annexation. She knew nothing of the particulars but learned that apart from the "generous" donation of land for new schools, the plan was for the City of Dubuque to not only annex the land parcel, but to literally enlarge the city in that direction. If voters approved, citizens would have a monstrous tax levy to pay for the so-called improvements! Being familiar with such devious devices perpetrated by parasitic individuals, I prepared a list of the many expenses that would have to come out of the pockets of the Dubuque tax payers. As I recall, my list included twenty-nine items which would be required to "improve" the city's new annexation; there was to be a mass meeting in protest that week. I was asked to attend and to read my list, and I did just that, describing the expenses for not only building a highway approach, power, lighting, sewers, all the sundry items – police, fire protection and so on! I paused after reading a last item, then asked: "Ladies and gentlemen, who will pay for the dog catcher?" That brought the meeting to an abrupt explosion of protest. Of course, the annexation was soundly defeated – someone suggested that I be nominated for Honorary Mayor!

A project for *Progressive Architecture* magazine in June 1966 was the photography of the Salk Institute in La Jolla by Louis Kahn. It was a pre-completion assignment to show how architect Louis Kahn related his design to the construction and techniques of concrete use in this one-of-a-kind institution. During the initial walk-around with the resident architect, it became apparent to me that Kahn possessed a sensitive understanding of the nature of concrete, and its contribution to the structure's appearance on completion, which

Bank of London, 1967
Testa, Elia, Ramos Architects, Buenos Aires, Argentina

223

Jonas Salk Institute of Biological Studies, 1966
Louis I. Kahn, La Jolla, California, 1959–66

combined to produce its innovative qualities. Observing the compass points of the sun's orientation, my procedure was quickly established. There was no genuine need to ask questions of the architect. My own assemblage of design concepts resulted in compositions which are of continued use to writers researching the basic elements; the reason for *Progressive Architecture*'s request for an analysis of the concrete's use. Although current requests are for photographs of the completed complex, I am happy when I receive comments on the 1966 construction technique scenes' serving as meaningful illustrations. As one writer indicated in his response to my submission: "Your photographs more than fulfill my needs!" I did no other photographs of the completed project after my original and only essay.

My first visit to Quebec province with editor Dan MacMasters of the *Times Home Magazine* was in 1968. We were producing a story in Montreal and its suburbs. Well armed with information and arrangements with architects, we were transported from home to home, each presenting a widely differing design. Following the publication of the *Home Magazine's* presentation of the above projects, with the enthusiastic reception by its readers and the Canadian Tourist Bureau representatives, we returned to Quebec province to expand our exploration, with major focus on the city of Quebec. The coverage included a refurbished 1609 house on the Ile d'Orleans on the St Laurence River.

Learning of my skiing activities, the Canadian officials invited me to their choicest ski areas in the Laurentian Mountains, north of

Montreal. The package included a first class flight from Los Angeles, a gourmet dinner on the evening of my arrival at Montreal featuring local specialities in a devastatingly delightful array which kept me and my host captivated for almost three hours. (The Fumé Blanc was a rare experience.) Montreal's Director of Tourism, my host, Monsieur Boissiere, described the prospects of my week's stay in the Laurentians. The next morning I was escorted to a lodge in the heart of the vast ski area. A member of the area ski patrol was my guide and hostess. She introduced me to the magic of powdered slopes on mountains with interlocking ski lifts enabling one to navigate full circle back to our lodge. I could not have experienced more ideal conditions. My skiing has carried me to many slopes including Europe and South America. But the uniqueness of the Laurentians lay in their elevation. The highest peak, Mt Tremblant, is only 3000 feet in elevation and the drop of the runs is close to sea level. By comparison, on California's Mammoth Mountain, 11,485 feet elevation hardly equals a similar drop! That plus the comfort of low altitude skiing precluded the need to become acclimatized to two mile high peaks. In glorious weather, I was photographing as we traversed the slopes, with my guide as a perfect model. I presented a complete set of the scenes to the mountain area's association and another to my Canadian Tourist Bureau's Montreal friend.

My continuing Canadian episodes brought another rewarding surprise. The *Los Angeles Times* had been so successful in promoting Canada that the Canadian Tourist Bureau representative for the L.A. area, on learning that I was attending the 1968 American Institute of Architecture National Convention in Boston, Massachusetts, called one day to ask: "Have you ever been to Nova Scotia?" Apparently the successes of our productions stemmed from the appeal to potential visitors of our observations of Canadian lifestyles – not of the usual lavishly flamboyant resort examples, but rather a reflection of the reality, what a visitor could readily garner in the exploration of a city's urban environment or its outlying countryside. The Bureau was highly appreciative. Our Nova Scotia excursion was a genuine postman's holiday for my wife and me. From the AIA Boston convention we drove to Portland, Maine where we boarded the Blue Nose ferry for a six-hour cruise in the Captain's station, to Yarmouth, the port at the southwestern tip of Nova Scotia. We were hailed at the pier by two men, one dangling a set of keys to a new Chrysler Sedan, our transportation for the exploration of the island. The Tourist Bureau representative had arranged our program – no

Jonas Salk Institute of Biological Studies, 1966
Louis I. Kahn, La Jolla, California, 1959–66

time limit, with an itinerary along the picturesque eastern coast, its fishing villages, secluded coves and inlets. We were to be put up in a series of inns and appear on local television stations every night during the newscasts: The usual "How do you like Nova Scotia?" interviews. My responses primarily expressed our admiration of the scenic beauty of the jagged coastline, and as an architectural photographer my pleasant reaction to the uniquely designed homes and the orderly nature of the towns and villages along the way!

Accustomed to the usual hasty driving of tourists in their rush to get from "point A to point B", our hosts in Sydney, at the north eastern edge of Nova Scotia, had become alarmed. It had taken us two weeks to cover the 200 miles. But we were made welcome with the key to the city and all the ingredients for a visiting dignitary as presented on television interviews. I congratulated the Scotians for their firm resolve: A respect for the blessings of Nature – and no signboards anywhere beyond city limits!

I trace my association with Nature to my early childhood on a farm in eastern Connecticut. Much of my feeling of well-being seems to have been generated there! This innermost association with Nature is basic. It is reflected in my photography on the slopes of Mount Tremblant and the shores of Nova Scotia. I did not just photograph skiers schussing down slopes; they are closely linked in my compositions with the glories of the mountain. Nor did I only "shoot" crashing waves on Nova Scotia shores.

After a brief stay in Sydney, including an off-shore visit to underwater iron ore deposits – the mainstay of Sydney's economy – we embarked for a flight to Montreal. There we boarded the Canadian Pacific's train across Canada to Vancouver on the west coast. But the surprise bonus, was an invitation to ride in the cab of the diesel engine as we departed from Calgary and ascended the Canadian Rocky Mountains – a photographer's delight of rugged canyons and peaks, long stretches of track through river valleys and tunnels bored in the depths of mountain ranges. On receiving my color photographs, the accolades were gratifying – and the engineering feats of last century's construction marvels were revealed wherever I pointed my camera. All of the endless days of adventure were devoid of uncertainty – the organization was so perfect and I never ran out of film. Several agencies of the government received the full package of my photographic work for that entire trip, and made full use of the pictorial representations as observed through the eyes of a traveling cameraman.

Top left and right:
Simard Residence, 1968
Esteril, Canada

Bottom left and right:
D. Lussier Residence, 1968
Montreal, Canada

229

Killingsworth House, 1966
Edward Killingsworth, Long Beach, California, 1966

By the time I photographed the house of architect Edward Killingsworth in 1966, I had recorded scores upon scores of houses since meeting architect Richard Neutra in 1936: Tiny, austere, scantily furnished and mostly minimal. Continuing projects also included numbers of houses of great dimensions. But too many of them were devoid of spirit; lacking what could be defined, in human terms, as personality. To measure in terms of plan, siting, decor and landscaping, one must discard opinionated observations. This Killingsworth house, as I review my 62 year career evaluations, stands in the forefront. It is not to be interpreted as an expression of "style", whichever one is chosen. Nor, in this instance, did Killingsworth attempt to "prove", to label; but rather he desired to

create spaces for a well defined structure in which his lifestyle would flourish. In this connection I should like to express my thoughts on the essence of what constitutes the definition of successful, even great architecture.

Years ago, while walking on a golf course in Yucca Valley, a desert region of Southern California, a dead leaf caught my eye. Intrigued by its skeletal structure, I carefully carried it to my car. At my studio I photographed it, associating the pattern of its "veins and arteries" with that of an urban development's design potential. I used an imposing enlargement for exhibits and a 35mm slide in my lectures on urban design to students, architects and professionals, creating a positive impact: few had ever been exposed to the realism

Right:
Learning urban planning from nature: A dry leaf, found in Yucca Valley, California

of the analogy! The above graphic parallel between Nature's form and urban development sparked a lively discussion. Audiences participated in accepting my contention: that the major "arteries" of the leaf portrayed boulevards and primary highways; the veins and capillaries demonstrated secondary byways and connecting thoroughfares. Apparently we can learn from Nature! Observe the leaf: it possesses a specific form endowed by Nature and within it is embodied an organized function embracing the entire body.

We humans, thrust into a maelstrom of so-called progress, orchestrated by greedy, self-serving "developers" and supported by irrational political emissaries are swept into their shallow schemes. The form of the leaf is distorted, mangled beyond reality. The direction to take, they say, is to expand: to create more jobs by enlarging our boundaries by annexing neighboring spaces. Fortunately there are communities which have learned by persevering; by demonstrating the genuine values ascribed to sound practices of restraint. For example, in an item in the *Los Angeles Times* of June 25, 1997 readers were told that the community of Thousand Oaks, California had created, pursued and achieved an idealistic plan. As with the boundary of a leaf's form, the plan for the community was executed as follows: "... they surrounded themselves with green, gathered it around the town's outskirts like a moat! A way to keep the San Fernando Valley's grinding urbanization at bay."

As a reprise to the above, a reminder: my comments on Dubuque, Iowa, demonstrate how it became possible for a community, as with the above Thousand Oaks "victory" over consuming short-sightness, to preserve a form of sanity in their control of their personal destiny. But I therefore plead: all citizens of a community should study my leaf!

Induced Perspectives

The chapter titled "My Beginnings" demonstrated my first works in photography. Those and my post-1934, 1935, and 1936 architectural photographs in Los Angeles of Neutra and Schindler houses were satisfactory but I soon realized how hampered I was by the lack of flexibility of my small camera, a vest-pocket Kodak. I acquired an old 4" x 5" camera and created "field trips" for practicing to learn the flexing of my new photographic "wings". Seeking a location where I could work undisturbed, I recalled the Neo-Renaissance buildings on the new University of California campus in Los Angeles. I had enrolled there as a freshman in 1929. I drove to the campus early on a Sunday morning, set up the camera and proceeded to make my first compositions. It was not too difficult, after a few attempts, to operate the camera movements and adapt them to the structure's forms. I had quickly observed how the primary function, avoiding the distortion of vertical elements of a building, could be resolved. I had preserved those 1937–38 negatives and had new prints made for this presentation.

During the following years I obtained a new camera, an Eastman Master View. It performed in fine style for many years. During a trip to Zurich in 1962, I met with Carl Koch, the originator of what became perhaps the most flexible and successful view camera in the history of photography. His Sinar camera systems provided formats, 4" x 5", 5" x 7", and 8" x 10". Koch had observed my photographs for years in many architectural publications. Our meeting offered the opportunity to exchange thoughts about creating effective and productive images of architecture. He suggested: "Would you like to use one of my cameras? I am certain its design qualities will surpass those of your 'old-style' equipment." A few weeks later, after my return to California, I received what appeared to me a "gold-plated" crate. It contained, not one, but two complete Sinar 4" x 5" cameras with lenses and attendant accessories. My hands quivered as I tore open each container.

As if operating an elegant scientific instrument, the Sinar turned my photographic life around. It performed, I believed, a continuing

Above:
My wife Emma and my Sinar, ca. 1960

Left:
McConnell Center, Pitzer College, 1969
Killlingsworth, Brady, Associates, Claremont, California, 1967

235

series of photographic miracles. My second book *The Photography of Architecture and Design,* in 1974, consisted almost entirely of Sinar photographs. I am including illustrations which depict the performances available with a sensitively maneuvered view camera. As a prime example, illustrated, it is not always possible to confront a building from a directly centered point of view. But architects frequently prefer a "head on" – so-called one-point perspective.

As an indication of the progression of technical advances in camera design, I experienced a rewarding incident after a lecture I presented at a Professional Photographers of America convention. I was approached by a representative of the Horseman Company of Japan. They were introducing their new view camera. I was invited to handle the demonstration model on the exhibit floor. Realizing that I had been a veteran Sinar proponent, I was shown the refinements of the Horseman; how movements were achieved with smooth turning of knobs compared to the more physical adjustments of my Sinar. Duly impressed, I couldn't help but express my delight. The representative asked me to wait a few moments – he had some phone calls to make. Soon he returned from his office, a broad smile on his face: "You now have a new Horseman camera. I informed the United States director of your response. All you should do is to write one of your magazine articles (which I did quite frequently for photography publications) using your new Horseman as you photograph a building of your choice. Would you, in the process, be explicit in referring to how you made 'before and after' exposures, with and without the camera's movements?" Within two weeks the equipment arrived. I covered an assignment immediately.

With each scene taken for my architect client I first made an exposure with all camera adjustments in neutral. That understandably recorded much that would not underline the client's needs. Without moving the camera, I then applied the movements on the Horseman which favorably refined the image of the scene as it would appear on the pages of books or magazines.

In retrospect, I now can pose questions. One observes in these times of highly technical advances in camera design, published photographs of inferior, distorted views of structures. I am concerned: is it a lack of judgment on the part of art editors and art directors, or are the assigned photographers ill-cast in their lack of proper equipment or experience? Where, furthermore, does the architect fit into a poor, misleading representation which does not honestly reflect his skills and talents?

I have been engaged in extensive programs and seminars which also develop into workshops for architects and photographers in many areas. An example: for nine years I had conducted continuing education programs at Iowa State University's School of Architecture. Collaborating with Eino Kainlauri, supervising and structuring the events, the results were rewarding for the participants. The primary aim of the programs concentrated on the definitive cognizance of a structure's design, thus offering an informative reading of the plan, siting and execution. Although most of the participants in the continuing education program used 35 mm

Lake Shore Drive Apartments, 1963
Ludwig Mies van der Rohe, Chicago, Illinois, 1948–51

237

Stuhr Museum of Pioneer Art, 1967
Edward Durell Stone, Grand Island, Nebraska,
1967

cameras, we suggested acquiring one of the "shift" lenses available. That was a fundamental need for the lens made it possible to use the camera just as "rising front" is used on a view camera. It would avoid distortion when a camera is tilted.

Each of my cameras in their contribution to the progression of my equipment refinements produced landmark photographs. Each was vital in my growth of perception. The resulting experiences were constant, no matter what camera was on my photographic stage; every decade represented an enrichment of a profound nature. I felt my stature growing. The evolution from the Eastman Master View to the Sinar and then to the Horseman came about in an orderly productive fashion. Perhaps I could liken that to the photographic process realized when exposures are taken with various films in black and white, color negatives and transparencies of each scene. Then the changing for 35mm color slides with another camera and differently rated film was achieved seemingly without a second thought. Those ongoing "expeditions" of picture-taking were reinforced by my earliest avoidance of instruments. When I purchased an exposure meter, a Weston I, in 1936, I quickly (and wisely) realized that it would derail my ability to literally "read" light; to switch my mental gymnastics in adapting my exposures to whatever film I was using. I discarded the meter before its first year of use.

To this day I plead with photographers: learn the values of whatever film is being used. Contribute to your store of under-

238

standing of light, artificial or natural. Contrary to this doctrine lies a trap: too many photographers, personal and professional, for their 35mm performances rely upon automatic cameras, no focusing, no exposure concern and, of course, no brains.

Light must be respected as the primary tool of photography. Photographers must realize that textures, forms, color, scale, are all specific products of light control and represent the manifestation of the ideal in a photograph. Therefore all the above experiences of camera transition were not idle physical entities. The achieved photographs mirror a growing, a maturing judgmental ability to produce images which transcend the commonplace.

In my pursuit of a more refined and accurate objective photograph, I am suggesting the application of what could be described as the ultimate in view camera use: the means of retaining true forms of perspective by reproducing accurately rectangular forms of a structure. The examples are of the Stuhr Museum of Pioneer Art in Grand Island, Nebraska by the architect Edward Durell Stone, 1967. The photograph, a fully "one-point" head-on demonstration, was taken early in the morning to capture the sweeping diagonal shadow of the roof and the sky-filled cloud formation; together with an optical effect of the pavement lines, all combine to form a statement of specific value. Later that morning, I observed an alternative scene. That introduced the water not visible in the first view but important to the architect. Moving the camera to that position, without using

Stuhr Museum of Pioneer Art, 1967
*Edward Durell Stone, Grand Island, Nebraska,
1967*

its correction facility, the building would have appeared to be tilted. By swinging the back of the camera, parallel with the plane of the building, the appearance reflected that of the first scene.

Another significant interpretation involves a view of the building's front as seen from a side perspective. My preferred camera position caused an up-sweep of the roof line. The roof line was restored to a horizontal visual correctness by swinging the back. Whereas there was little doubt as to the veracity of the previous two corrected examples, this particular view, when presented to the architect, offered a choice: "Even though the uncorrected view is more dramatic in its almost over-powering the true form of the corrected view, I therefore select for the sake of consistently depicting the rectangular nature of the scene."

My photographic life has been permeated with a concern for replicating the visual phenomena of perspective. The history of art from remote ages indicates one of the difficulties confronting artists: were the early creators of expressions lacking in their understanding of the need for "inducing" perspective on their rock walls, or other available surfaces? The absence of perspective in primitive works is not necessarily deliberate. The forms of life on the walls of caves recounted actual life confrontations; therefore, perspective did not occur. But within my experiences, camera in hand, my observations resulted from the assembly of lines and forms. Transferring, in turn, from my visuals to film was nothing more than a tripping of the camera's shutter!

On viewing my photographic imaging of induced perspectives I recognized the "ingredients" which were involved in the instrumentation of the scenes assembled either on my camera's viewer or ground glass screen. Apparently I gave little thought to a premeditated concept of more than a spontaneous assembling of lines and forms. But during the recent reviewing of my archival excerpts there dawned a realization that within the construction of compositions, elements of perspective were significant.

The two gate photographs illustrate non-associable values. The gate of a school scene on the Caribbean island of St Thomas is one-dimensional; a wrought-iron framework which creates a perspective of eye-leading lines. The contrived perspective, albeit the flat gate elements, in reality, is associated with the complex activities of the school children in the background. The second gate scene is an idealized framework of perspective affirmation. Note that I selected an off-center camera positioning, favoring the wider portion of the

gated structure to the left. That reinforced the black pavement lines beginning with the one which touches the gate at the left, thus heightening the impact as the four black lines culminate at the steps. However, as I viewed this scene before setting my view camera, I must have been attracted to the spaces beyond the steps. That the Baron Rothchild Memorial occupied the distant wooded area was obvious; but my selection of the lineal elements which guided my assembly of "visual acoustics" apparently worked for me in the construction of my composition.

By minimalizing the fourth black line at the right, using the shortened gate area to act as a shield, I induced a powerful line at the left. The Rothchild escutcheon above the open gate invites the viewer to associate with the entire scene – considerably before arriving at the memorial. This photograph was achieved almost forty years ago, but at this moment in my life it gives me considerable joy to think that I created a companion to other statements which may assist others in pursuit of vivid achievements with the camera.

My University of Southern California perspective with only one line and a lamp post constitutes a variation of the Memorial essay. Could it qualify for a "less is more" identity in its simplification of the "laws" of perspective? I'm certain that Mies van der Rohe would

Above:
School gate in St Thomas, 1986

Right:
Baron de Rothschild tomb, Israel, 1959

242

agree. Applying this qualification to my exercise at an A. C. Martin's office building in a one-point perspective's construction, it can be accepted as a valid dimensional reference. By maintaining a positive horizontality at the far end of the space, the composition's left area diagonal establishes a form of perspective. Is not this reminiscent of the above statements: placing perspective into a functional role so that the reading of a photograph is more palpable? Far afield from the photographs described is the factory scene. My assignment, to illustrate the features of a sophisticated chemical-conveying pipe plant, suggested a provocative subject. That it was, but finding a 16" x 20" print in my old file, I was delighted to observe that it would fit into my induced perspectives essay. When I took the photograph, I was attracted to the dimensional quality of the pipes which protruded towards my camera. At this writing, intrigued with analyzing perspectives in my photographs, I can realize how the pipe scene's portrayal of the subject is exactly right in its "collaboration" with the others. Finally, I discovered another enticing demonstration which envelopes the ingredients of my exploration into a too often

Department of Water and Power, 1965
A. C. Martin Associates, Los Angeles, California, 1965

243

disregarded element of illustration: a rack of glass discs at a mirror silvering company. When they were illuminated by floodlights, a startling effect was created. A series of repetitive circles appeared. That "induced" a form of perspective not evident in my other photographs. Furthermore, the sharp-edged discs delineated by my lighting produced an effect, as if the circles of reflectancy were floating beneath and into the glass discs. In reality the induced, non-existent images were ghosts: they penetrated the pure circular forms of the glass discs. The president of the company requested a huge blow-up of the photograph to hang on a wall in his office. It mystified most of his visitors!

For my personal satisfaction, as I have been reviewing my photography, almost from day one, uncovering the consistency of my compositions and my sensitivity to light has become a source of genuine joy. In 1934, for example, with my Vest Pocket Kodak, I

Left:
Pacific Tube Company, 1953

Right:
Olin Hall, University of Southern California, 1963
William Pereira Associates, Los Angeles, California, 1963

recognized the textural lighting on the University of California's Life Science Building in Berkeley, California. Five years later, as a professional in Los Angeles, on assignment in 1939 to photograph a new department store, my visual response was identical. The textural prominence of the material on the facade was similar to the 1934 building. My two photographs exhibited that feature, indicating the consistency of my approach. Perhaps Frank Lloyd Wright, in later years of acquaintanceship, recognized my inbred sensitivity. Richard Neutra, for so many decades of spirited association also felt it. As

Dione Neutra often put it, "Richard is so happy with your photography's respect for his design." I cannot resist those expressions. I can only convey the personal satisfaction and dividends when my photography produces, as expressed by editors and architects, a quintessential statement of design achievement. The only requirement for photographers, is to open their minds and eyes upon viewing a structure.

A forceful demonstration: Architects Anshen & Allen of San Francisco had designed a high-rise office building of significant and innovative detailing. Their International Building was widely published; national magazines assigning photographers for that purpose. Sadly, as related to me in later years, although featured extensively, the photographs failed to portray the primary designs. Apparently the requirement was to observe how and at what time of day those features would be detailed. But on the cover of one of the magazines the selected photograph completely failed to indicate the detail responsible for the editors' publications.

But this "neglect of duty" on the part of the various photographers had a happy ending. I was assigned to photograph the building for a major glass company to advertise the unique fenestration and attendant qualities of the required installation of the glass. Architects Anshen and Allen recounted their ensuing reactions to the event after receiving a set of my photographs from the glass company. They both had been subjected that particular day to a series of crises. Late in the afternoon a secretary placed the package of my photographs on one of their desks. With shouts and cheers they assembled their staff. Steve Allen, one of the principals, described the occasion. With my photographs laid out on their conference table, they placed the magazines which had published the buildings in the center of the display.

In the midst of the derisive condemnations of the publications, Allen called me to express his joy. All the burdens of the day's problems evaporated; they were going home to arrange a family dinner outing to celebrate their redemption. After all, as Allen stated, International Building was the most prominent contract they had ever executed. The magazines, although generous in their platitudes, had failed in their assigned photographers' disregard for the intrinsic physical exercises in design. Apart from receiving assignments for the firm's major projects henceforth, the occasion of

International Building, 1962
Anshen and Allen, San Francisco, California, 1962

almost electrifying the entire firm provided an invaluable service to all. Anshen and Allen sent a comment to the magazines together with a sampling of my "glorious" photographs.

In tripping my camera shutter, one of the great rewards in photography can be recognized. It relates to the moment. Unless the sunlight/shadow phenomenon in the delineation of structures and their materials is observed and applied, the photographer may fail in the recording of values which create the dimensional aspects of a photograph. The purpose of "the moment" is to project the process of communicating with the best possible art. What I had applied in my photography is expressed. The emphasis, at the onset of absorbing the concept, "the best possible art," is conveyed in an often related query from viewers of my photography: "Your subjects do not move, you have lots of time."

Not true! To capture "the moment," a fleeting glimpse of a desired effect may exist as the sun moves onto or through a building's surface. Therefore, much to the astonishment of those in the area of my work, I sometimes activate my exposures with speed as if I were photographing a sport event!

The moment applies to a surprising number of projects, often under unexpected circumstances. One puzzled me, for I had been photographing the Camino Real Hotel in Mexico City for architect Ricardo Legoretta. In the process of inspecting the lobby with its endless stream of guests, I realized that the only time for a minimal tide of traffic would be at an extremely early hour. To demonstrate what could be construed as a fortunate accident, I observed during an early review, that I would require a number of my lights to illuminate the expansive multi-formed space. However when I entered the lobby even at an earlier hour the following morning, the sunlight which had been blocked by clouds the preceding day was flooding a walled area of the hotel's courtyard. In turn the reflected light penetrated the glass-walled lobby, flooding the entire area. The "fortunate aspect?" The lobby's ceiling, a multi-faceted design, would have been extremely difficult to illuminate uniformly. Together with the required complexity of lighting the entire lobby, as it appeared during my previous day's inspection, I would have been confronted with a tediously labored task. But the unexpected bonus was that the light reflected from the courtyard was more perfect than I could ever have imagined. The scene indicates how the blessing of a cloudless morning with my instant moment of grasping the situation enabled me to achieve another winner. Architect Legoretta at his initial

viewing of the photograph appeared to be puzzled: "How did you light up the ceiling?" I used not one of my many light reflectors.

Although it was not a moment requiring the speed of a sports photograph, this widely-published photograph's impact could not have been achieved if I had not grasped the opportunity of Nature's assistance. I conclude this detailed dissertation with a comment: yes, it is gratifying to be at the right place at the right time. But the observation attendant to that situation is elementary also. What is the next step, finding oneself confronted by the "situation"?

When I embarked upon the photography of architecture career, certainly there were no guidelines. But can ensuing generations of photographers and architects assimilate the substance of my evaluations which hopefully would upgrade a profession's standards? Right from the start, even with my *Track Meet* photo of 1927, I

Above and overleaf:
Hotel Camino Real, 1981
Ricardo Legoretta, Mexico City, Mexico, 1968

249

apparently recognized that my viewing of a scene was wholly of my own choosing. It followed naturally, that when architects would conduct me through a project to show me what they had in mind, leading the way, they would often walk past certain elements which caught my attention, as offering specific definitive views. Not realizing that I had stopped to discuss a composition with my assistant, the architect would even disappear into another area.

I learned that it was not unusual for architects to be incapable of placing their own design statements on film. During my workshops in Continuing Education programs, it was evident that architects' training in the visual arts was sorely lacking. In the preparation and exploration for associating my life with architectural values, I concluded that it would be wise to perform hands-on communicating. As an example, architect Albert Frey, possessing a strong ability to evaluate his designs, envisioned a photograph of his aluminum-clad home in Palm Springs as best taken in the morning. But my suggested analysis, with its turreted cylindrical form springing out of the completed print, was a shocking surprise. The minute textures of the aluminum would not have been revealed had the scene been attempted in the morning. My mid-afternoon composition has been widely published and exhibited throughout the world.

Another incidence of how light balance can offer a perfect representation of the way a building relates to its landscaping and the siting is my photograph of Richard Neutra's Moore residence in Ojai, California. First of all, the composition entailed capturing the late afternoon textured lighting on the distant hills. Then I recognized the penetrating sunlight from window areas at the western wall of the house. However, to establish a complete statement, the dark wood-formed ceiling, not receiving the afternoon sunlight, required carefully positioned auxiliary lighting. The resultant image actually echoed the landscape, ranging to infinity.

Another example of utilizing sunlight in a selected moment is my study of architect Edward Killingsworth's Case Study House grouping "Triad" in which favorable conditions provided a means of assembling an appealingly dramatic formation of Killingsworth's straightforward architecture. By observing when the moment of maximum sunlight penetration prevailed on the house's forms and creating a camera statement to make a play on the delightful reflection in the pond, the viewer experiences a two-pronged situation: as the path from the left meets the steps, their reflection carries the

Case Study House #23, 1960
Killingsworth, Brady and Smith, La Jolla,
California, 1960

eye into the water to embrace the house reflection. But up the steps the house is "entered".

As I pen these experiences I have grasped the significance of thoughtfulness in the camera's (and photographer's) role in the positioning of art forms in architectural photography. Somehow I cannot express that statement too seriously. Perhaps my activities can be likened to a child's playing with building blocks! That, I am certain, occurred when I was producing another Killingsworth essay, his Duffield automobile agency in Long Beach, California.

As usual, anticipating the positioning of shadows generated by the sunlight, I calculated the precise moment at which the wall would be bisected by the post's and wall's shadow. Sensing the need for a figure I enlisted the aid of the company's attractive secretary. But I sent her back for her handbag. After all, I suggested, she was to enact the role of a rich client purchasing a Lincoln motor car. Her position against the blank wall was perfect in establishing scale. Finally, the completion of my form and line statement was indicated by the left turn of the concrete lawn curbing as it met the bottom of my composition.

My photograph of an indoor/outdoor living space at Ocho Cascadas (eight cascades or waterfalls) in Puerto Vallarta, Mexico also demonstrates how my compositional approach addressed the situation in terms of light. Architect Edward Giddings' familiarity with climate and weather in the area precluded the need of physical enclosures for most of his spaces. The selected point of view, I decided, would appeal to viewers; but only if I were to determine exactly how much sunlight should penetrate the area. As the light crept up the wall on the right side, the proportion of light and shade governed my decision as illustrated. I directed the two subjects for an attitude of relaxed conversation.

The balancing of interior and exterior lighting to create visual continuity between architectural elements is perfectly achieved in the Ocho Cascadas scene. Not all of my requirements have been met so naturally. Observe my photograph of a scene at the Kona Surf Hotel in Hawaii. The hotel's public relations director had requested a "picture of the room". Mostly, in P.R. parlance, the photograph would have been taken with no indication of more than perhaps a glimpse of the balcony.

By placing my camera on the threshold, the bedroom, balcony, plus the architecture of the entire structure is revealed. Actually, the far end echoes my camera's opposite situation. To achieve the

Duffield's Lincoln-Mercury Showroom, 1963
Killingsworth, Brady and Smith, Long Beach, California, 1963

257

Ocho Cascadas, 1980
Edward Giddings, Puerto Vallarta, Mexico,
1980

259

Kona Surf Hotel, 1972
*Hawaii Architects, Associates, Keauhou, Hawaii,
1972*

lighting balance, I had waited for the afternoon sun to strike the foreground balcony and the entire western facade of the hotel. To create an extension of the sunlight into the room, I mounted a light at the far end of the draperied window wall. Another foreground light filled the balance of the room. To equal the exterior intensity of daylight, two blue flashbulbs were used in my reflectors.

When this photograph was presented, with a scream of delight, the P. R. lady reached for her telephone; alerted the printing company that an "important" new photograph was to be featured on the cover! Its caption: "You get the entire hotel when you occupy one of our rooms!" The photograph so impressed the editor of a hotel trade journal that he published a suggestion to hotel owners: "Utilize the services of a professional architectural photographer as an assurance that you receive this quality as representative of your hotel's amenities!" A large imprint of the scene was included.

For newcomers to photography, be they amateur or professionally inclined in some future period, the beginnings can be simplified. Observe the passing moments of sunlight, how images change. I strongly suggest: learn to observe the properties of light; photograph shadow-created images.

A Reservoir of Photographs

With continuing research and processing of my archives, new appraisals emerge in my thoughts: the role in my career as a communicator of information. Do my interpretations of architecture express what the public and editors do not usually see? For example, the auditorium in Carlyle, Pennsylvania serves as a demonstration of interpretive architectural photography. Frequently, in assuming my often experienced role as a "provider", as a major source of illustrations for design publications and books, I have found myself adapting an insistent attitude. My photographs not only mirrored the physical, but also attributed to what generally was unseen. My ability to fathom the depths of a design and record it created a transcendental visual product.

A publisher recently sent a list of photographs, interiors and exteriors, for a publication of a decade's expressions. He had obtained the "list" by perusing other books. Instead of complying, I submitted my choices, mostly scenes of the identical structures, but not widely published. They served to identify the designs without aping the previous widely-published views. In my cover letter I wrote, "I was there and lived the designs as I composed my statements." The outcome of this incident was that a major number of my presentations in black and white and color were published. The person delegated to contact me had no concept of procedure; she assumed that the list, not having a reference to other possibilities, was the instrument with which to contact me. My color scenes, many of which were reproduced on full and double pages, were a significant enhancement to the book's marketability. If I had adhered to the original request, the contents of the proposed volume would have echoed similar illustrations previously published elsewhere. But instead, the new book had a breath of freshness with so many of my rarely-published photographs. We actually expanded the communication of quality architectural and interior designs.

A typical "abandoned" project uncovered during my exploration of archives is represented by two color photographs of a project I did at the home of sculptor and designer Mathias Goeritz while visiting

Harder House, 1980
Bruce Goff, Mountain Lake, Minnesota, 1979

Mexico in 1973. This presentation demonstrates how designer Goeritz enjoyed playfully using a palette of brilliant colors to structure the delineation, as in the wall-sidewalk relationship. I recall taking a photograph as I observed a family, a mother and two children, approaching Goeritz' house and stepping off the sidewalk which he had painted and moving on to the street to avoid stepping on the colored area. As a relief against the dazzling yellow wall I "inserted" Goeritz to provide scale, stepping into the interior; the art and other components lend a light touch to the space.

For his January 23, 1977 issue of the *Washington D.C. Star's Home/Life* supplement, editor James W. Toland had discussed with me, during a meeting in his office in early 1976, his idea for a widely-ranged story on the vast choices this country offers for the enjoyment of our geographic and environmental diversity. This was to include the importance of selecting quality architects who would be sympathetic to the client's programs as well as relating to the site development.

I suggested that in my nation-wide assignment "excursions," I had either photographed or had listed many story ideas. When editor Toland and I reviewed my projects, we speedily agreed on a selection. All four are of designs by prominent architects, serving clients' needs with utmost sensitivity. The four selected houses were a desert abode in Palm Springs, California, the Donner Lake ski chalet in Northern California, central Iowa's remote Lake McBride as the site for an ideally situated year-round retreat and, finally, a multi-level residence fronting the wildly dramatic Pacific coastline at Carmel, California. I had photographed three of the four prior to 1976, visiting Iowa in the Fall to avoid the heavy shadows created by the giant oak trees when in full leaf. Although three of our choices were situated in California, other areas of the country could have provided equally effective situations. Certainly Colorado's Rocky Mountains in winter or summer offer locales for vacation houses as excitingly dramatic as California or even the Swiss Alps. And Maine's "rocky shoreline" could echo the scene in the Carmel, California setting. Scattered throughout the United States are thousands of lake-fronted retreats. Iowa was selected as a mid-country demonstration of disciplined design in a relaxing, practical location. Of course, the desert of Palm Springs with its unique house by architect William Cody was an immediate choice for such a site.

Technically, the primary photographic need is to insure that the staged interior lighting produces a subtle balance with the intensity

Left and above:
Goeritz Residence, 1973
Mathias Goeritz, Cuenavaca, Mexico, 1972

Overleaf:
La Estadia Development, 1981
Ricardo Legoretta, Mexico City, Mexico, 1981

of the exterior, whether it is a brilliant ocean front or a soft early evening effect in a snow oriented structure. Therefore, the purpose was to reproduce the specific mood of each of the four houses.

Each design was chosen as a demonstration of how the architect responded to the client's and nature's role in the function of the home. The Carmel, California house is a perfect example of how the intense afternoon sunlight was used to great effect: the sweeping roof line became, in effect, a visor-like device as it performed its role as a sun shield. The owner, a writer, duly relished the site's daytime visual amenities, while loving the security of the durable stone walls of his study on strong winter nights. Even the force of the winds was diminished with the double-glazing of the windows. Designer John Howard Gamble respected the elements: the warmth of late afternoon winter sun plus the security of the above "stone-walled" space.

Within an area of vivid contrast, not unrelated, is architect William Cody's desert home. Here too, the late afternoon sun's often scorching temperatures demand the shelter of the twelve-foot roof extension to the west. Whereas the ocean-oriented house was obliged to perform within a wide range of nature's demands as reflected by the comforting enclosures of space, the desert home welcomed the indoor-outdoor aspects of living as displayed; the cool quarry-tiled floor and the glass wall as a welcome to the expansive views to the west, culminating in the over 10,000-foot high San Jacinto Mountains.

Although displayed here as a winter activity setting, the formidable Buff and Hensman-designed Sierra Nevada mountain retreat also responds favorably to summer activities. The extended roof's structure becomes a dual-purpose device: on the exterior it hovers over the entry while serving for the interior as a visual protection from sky glare for the 18-foot high center of the structure's generous heart. This shelter-like abode was selected as one of the foursome for its wide interplay – the architects' ability and inclination to extend their basic space evaluations to encompass the aspect of the client's

Above and left:
Cody Residence, 1963
William Cody, Palm Springs, California, 1963

Overleaf:
Gorman House, 1973
John Howard Gamble, Carmel, California, 1973

269

living-activity modes. To me, acclimatized by my long associations with "total design" in my photography, it was a rewarding experience to relate to such thorough statements.

When I review my photographs of Ray Crites' lake-front house in Iowa, I remember the story of his house. The owners changed their original version of it as a vacation "escape" to that of a full-time residence. The encompassing perfection of the house fulfilled the family's living style, so they did not have to wait. They decided to make this delicious house their permanent residence.

In reviewing my photography of the Rufino Tamayo Museum in Mexico City, 1981 and the photography assignment I did of the home of Rufino Tamayo for the *Los Angeles Times Home Magazine* in 1973 with editor Dan MacMasters, one can see how varied two assignments can be for coverage on the same subject, the artist and his museum. We were to photograph the home of Mexico's brilliant artist, to illustrate his lifestyle including scenes which would show personal preferences of his work. Having been alerted that he was camera-shy, I composed a scene in Tamayo's living room in which I had placed him in the position of viewing a mirror on a wall. I suggested that he look at my camera, which was reflected in the mirror, and the resultant image captured a comfortable expression of the painter. He hardly realized that he had been photographed. His reflection in the mirror was the key to a successful portrait.

The presentation of the Tamayo Museum will serve the purpose of illustrating the varied projects confronting an architectural photographer during the course of his daily work. The renowned Mexican artist, Rufino Tamayo, throughout his great and internationally acclaimed career, amassed a volume of brilliant works. Fellow Mexican architect, Abraham Zabludovsky, undertook to design a suitable structure to house the collection.

Because of Mexico's susceptibility to violent earthquake activity, those seismic forces were addressed with utmost concern for stable architectural and engineering collaboration. It would appear, at the initial viewing of Zabludovsky's design for the Tamayo, that elements

Below:
Resort House, 1976
Buff and Hensman, Donner Lake, California, 1973

Left:
Shive Residence, 1962
Ray Crites, Solon, Iowa, 1962

Overleaf:
Garcia House, 1975
John Lautner, Los Angeles, California, 1962

Above:
The artist Rufino Tamayo, 1973

Right:
Rufino Tamayo Museum, 1981
Abraham Zabludovsky with Teodoro Gonzalez de Leon, Mexico City, Mexico, 1981

of incongruity or imbalance were present; why was it necessary to house art works in what appeared as an overwhelming volume of massive beams and columns? It was apparent to me that to photograph with the above circumstances carefully considered, the scale of the predominant volumes of the spaces' structural forms were to be honored as the key to recognizing the total design and goals of the institution. True, if the photographic assignment was commissioned by an art publication to cover Tamayo's creations, it was likely that the photographic vocabulary would differ from that displayed in my works. Therefore, this assignment for the architect has reproduced three images: first of all, the architect's concepts; secondly, representation of Tamayo's art; and, thirdly, my interpretations. The latter represented how I reacted to the total imagery of the two individuals involved. On this project, as with all my previous assignments from Zabludovsky, he was in constant attendance. The compositions were mine, but before taking an exposure, I showed Zabludovsky a Polaroid print. Putting our heads together, we analyzed it, often making adjustments in the camera position of what would seem insignificant movements, yet this method of refining the statement spelled out how and why my photography literally distills architecture into a palatable summary of an achievement – an embodiment of design for a broad segment of our population.

Finally, I recall Zabludovsky's explanation of one highly dramatic scene which related the massive beams in my photograph to the total structure of the great hall. He had described how the spanning of the space was performed. The attendant photographs to this story were all-inclusive. The quality of the art and the architecture are well-related to each other and with thoughtful photography a composition of the entire project is completely expressed.

The sheer joy of my work is to be assigned to photograph a structure, knowing nothing whatsoever about it in advance. What a surprise to receive a telephone call from architect Walter Gropius in Cambridge, Massachusetts: "Would you please consider the photography of one of our firm's (The Architects Collaborative) newest projects?" I had met Gropius in his office previously and engaged in a prolonged conversation about our mutual involvement in architectural experiences.

The assignment was to photograph the Anita Tuvin Schlecter auditorium in Carlyle, Pennsylvania. I was to meet the project architect on a prescribed date. She explained the clients' program: to design an all-purpose structure, serving a wide range of functions:

Rufino Tamayo Museum, 1981
Abraham Zabludovsky with Teodoro Gonzalez de
Leon, Mexico City, Mexico, 1981

From lecture halls of customary sizes to a total occupancy of the space for major events as concerts and other total seating needs. The solutions to the complex requirements were portrayed during dual assignments, June and November, 1971. Not all the promised elements were completed when I arrived in June.

The keynote of the entire interior space assemblage was the incorporation of a new product of the Modern Fold Company, Inc. It consisted of flexible elements which were coiled vertically and withdrawn into receptacles for creating various spaces as required. The "coiled" walls were operated electrically, moved on tracks on the ceilings and floors. The walls were sound-proofed in their construction. My photographs were composed to demonstrate, in several sequences, the enlarging or diminishing of areas. That was controlled from an upper level glassed-in space. The area's windowed viewing lookout is visible from all the space elements of the floor levels below.

During my photographic sequences I saw to it that there was a continuity, making it possible to observe how each space was created. That process was made possible by the full cooperation of the auditorium's director. Also seated at the control room's panels, the operator could communicate with me in responding to my requests as determined by each composition. Furthermore, to facilitate lighting and the certainty that all the fixtures would function, I was accompanied by a technician.

The quality of the total available space would best be represented by a demonstration. "If only I could find enough students," I asked the director. In response, the next day after class periods a chamber music group, two pianists and an organist were present, and seated on the perimeter were members of the college choral groups! My plan was to have them simulate a concert. I was introduced and suggested that they perform "Shulman's Opus 1", a concerto for two pianos, organ, chamber ensemble and chorus. "Just make sounds to entertain yourselves while I take a few exposures." My camera had been stationed before the group's arrival. For my entertainment, the ensemble performed a bit of a Mozart Serenade, the choral group sang the college song, the pianos and organ sounded some chords and I achieved my "opus".

A delight to all, especially Gropius. It served as the primary demonstration of the auditorium's design. Just a bit of imagination and willingness to perform my "opus" produced an image that even the architects had never anticipated. I requested that the partitioned-

Anita Tuvin Schlecter Auditorium, 1971
The Architects Collaborative Inc., Carlyle,
Pennsylvania, 1971

Overleaf:
Burgess Residence, 1982
Albert Frey (Consultant), Palm Springs, California,
1981

off lecture hall with students in attendance, wait for a few moments for an exposure. That was taken the next day while the choral group and chamber ensemble were rehearsing. The sound-proofed partitions functioned perfectly. The above two scenes with occupancy could never have otherwise demonstrated the effective usage. The response from TAC on delivery of my completed photographs was gratifying, particularly since few of the group had ever seen the plans and drawings. Professionally they admired the clear "reading and continuity" between the areas.

During one of my meetings with Ansel Adams in the early 1980s, we had discussed my role in architectural photography. He referred to an acquaintance's suggestion that "I was the Ansel Adams of architectural photography." Would I, he asked, "conduct a workshop at Yosemite"? I responded favorably, for he and I in our close associations with nature experienced a common area of intentions. Yes, I would relate my program to "The Architecture of Nature" as the primary theme. The workshop was conducted in September, 1983, the year of Adams' death. His daughter-in-law, Jeanne Adams, served as the director. Yosemite's famed Ahwahnee Hotel, one of my favorite structures, was the centerpiece of the program for it represented in the designing experience by architect Underwood, in 1927, a positive kinship to our theme's Nature-Architecture intertwining. The photographs taken as elements of the workshop related the brilliant design of the structure to the magnificent mountains, cliffs and forests. We had no problem in orienting our compositions; the Architecture of Nature blended with every scene.

While preparing a series of future programs for workshops I experienced a disturbing incident. I had been invited to conduct a workshop for an association of photography instructors. They were of high school and college level and desired an exposure to "some of my expertise" on how to photograph architecture. Our first program, on the UCLA campus, was intended to demonstrate the introductory procedure; how to organize the thought process when coming upon a structure for the first time. When we met at an appointed time and place, the instructors all 45 of them, were prepared. Cameras of all sizes and shapes, 35 mm to a variety of 2 1/4" equipment. Also, an abundance of 4" x 5" view cameras. We had selected the Dickson Art Center by architect William Pereira. Its southern elevation design elements were ideal for a demonstration of their response to early morning south-eastern sunlight. Unfortuna-

Ahwahnee Hotel, 1981
Gilbert Stanley Underwood, Yosemite Village, California, 1927

tely, during my opening remarks I was confronted by a volume of shutter clickings. I asked the group, what they were doing and which they had chosen as their primary components. Obviously (to me) the shadows projected by the concrete fenestration were too broad. It would take another 20–30 minutes for the sun to move into a more southerly direction. This would have refined the shadow proportions, thereby producing a cleaner delineation of the entire design.

As I explained the process of perception, how a photographer could (or should) orient his vision so that when the camera is introduced, the resultant composition's statement would become easier to observe, there arose a murmuring of dissent from one of the instructors. He protested: "We came here to learn how to photograph a building, not to listen to a speech!" Fortunately he was shouted down by the group. "We are here just for that purpose, to learn to sharpen our perceptive and judgmental abilities." With a pair of before and after 4" x 5" Polaroids I was able to calm down the protestor.

What does this tell us? That a carefully scrutinized evaluation of a structure is the cardinal rule, and time is in favor of this procedure. So why not honor those great images which appear before us and abandon "grab-a-shot" tendencies. Good photography is a joy. It reflects man's ability to think, contemplate and reason! With a qualitative approach, we can learn to identify the innate properties of self. Then photography will not be a mystery. Instead, it becomes an extension of our spirit.

Dickson Art Center, University of California Los Angeles, 1983
William Pereira and Associates, Los Angeles, California, 1965

The Retirement Years

The Retirement Years

It is now the end of October, 1997. I have just returned from attending the annual American Institute of Architects Awards program of the Los Angeles Chapter. Flashing across large-screened projections were the proclaimed winners. With much applause, even cheering, the 750 architects, families, business and contracting associates, and clients expressed their approval and acceptance of the winners. Except me! During the past two years, in the process of relating my life's story of architectural associations for over 60 years, I have asked my friends: "What is all the cheering about?" With each projected image I became more and more morose. I envisaged the giants of the architectural world with whom I grew up as I photographed what are now regarded by many as genuine historical landmarks. This was not simply a case of "things were different in those days." The images of the Award winners frightened me. I shuddered as my vision became clouded by memories. I could attempt not to be opinionated. But entrenched in my own personal "winners" circles of the architecture in my life's span, I could only think of those whose dedication to their clients went hand in hand with their design directions. I recall my first meeting in 1963 with Walter Gropius. Seated in his Cambridge, Massachusetts office we spent hours exchanging thoughts. I remember distinctly, how he expressed his dedication to clients' programs. Later that day at his staff meeting there was a similar flow of fervent concern in their expressions towards the production of only the finest structures, executed for a world-wide clientele.

I did not recognize that quality in the works of the "winners". Their dissertations appeared to be directed towards an abstract play of forms, often touching on fantasy, reading into their designs elements which were not evident in the projected photographs. How far removed, I observed, from the designs of the winners in early Award programs. Those images portrayed the concerns of the architects for functionally appealing solutions without resorting to the abundant outpouring of architectural jazz prevalent these past decades.

Santa Anita Racetrack, 1938
Arcadia, California

Richard Neutra and me, 1950

I believe our only real hope lies with those architects who have not compromised the inherent spirit still existing among the masters of architecture. The works of the late John Lautner spring to mind. Originating his career after many years of association with Frank Lloyd Wright, his abundant, innovative designs reveal the greatness of the man! They bear witness to how an architect could evolve a design philosophy without insulting the judgment and good taste of the public. What a contrast between Lautner's ingenious creativity and the work of those in frantic pursuit of what I identify as "false-fronted facades".

In this connection, I recall reading of a communication between Frank Lloyd Wright and designer Paul Frankl, an Austrian emigre. Frankl became successful almost immediately upon his arrival in this country. He was in New York in 1928, writing a definitive book on the theme, "What is Modern?" Wright, in his letter, protested design directions and proposed a crusade for the cause of style against "Styles." Frankl was identified by Wright as "A 5th Avenue soldier on the front lines". Frankl, in the 1930s, moved to Los Angeles where he was highly successful with his designs of houses. His showroom on what is now exclusive Rodeo Drive, exhibited dramatically displayed furniture of his designs. He coincidentally was one of my earliest clients. Paul Laszlo's studios with his array of furniture designs were situated directly across Rodeo from Frankl.

Furthermore, as I perused voluminous writings of the earliest years of this century, a poignant observation was revealed. Referring to the newness of what today is marked as modernism, a writer summed up the movement: "Otto Wagner as the Godfather, Adolf Loos as a prophet, and Frank Lloyd Wright the Messiah!" Although Loos and Wagner lived during early decades, I learned considerably from Richard Neutra's accounts of their functions and philosophy; as a student in Vienna he had been deeply impressed by their designs. Those accounts were most often delivered by Neutra during our drives to distant assignments.

My extensive reading on the subject, my friendship with Frank Lloyd Wright and Neutra's eloquent evaluations of the early giants have provided me with a wealth of information often surpassing that of many students at schools of architecture. I beseech those genuinely seeking out the richness of our architectural heritage to spend more energy in researching history, thus avoiding temptations of the "newer" architects who continue to rise briefly above our horizons.

From the mid-1980s onwards, I became involved in unanticipated activities. Prior to my participation in the Museum of Contemporary Art's Case Study House program, I had received an invitation to conduct illustrated lectures at Vienna's Technische Hochschule (School of Architecture). It was to be co-sponsored by the United States Information Agency. The students, articulate and highly informed in their knowledge of worldwide architecture, engaged in lively discussions on the directions of design practices. My photography, occupying considerable space in their textbooks, was familiar to them. I did not come as a stranger!

A short time elapsed, again another call from Vienna's director of the Architects Center, Martin Boeckl. "We are organizing a program of considerable magnitude. Can you send photographs of the works of six emigres who left Vienna: Neutra and Schindler in 1920 and 1928; with the file material you may have on Victor Gruen, Paul Frankl, Rudy Baumfeld, and Liane Zimbler? We shall require prints for reproduction in a book and other larger ones for an exhibit in our Hall illustrating their achievements. Also, if you are willing, we would appreciate your appearance as a guest lecturer as a participant in our activities; to deliver an address on the state of architecture, as you had photographed it for the 'group'".

During the following years I was invited by the director of the Continuing Education Department of Iowa State University's School of Architecture in Ames, Iowa to conduct field trip seminars for architects, photographers and students. The program, coordinated under the direction of Eino Kainlauri, attracted fifty students from fourteen states. The series was extended for an additional eight years with visits to view, evaluate and discuss the photographic process of capturing the elements of design statements.

On all our visits, emphasis was placed on sharpening visual acuity. As a major consequence, perception was enlivened and students said: "We are beginning to see through our eyes with minds governing our actions!" Many of the group became adept at rendering designs of their own completed projects, observing compositions they had not visualized before!

One day I received a request from an old time client: "Have you saved prints and/or negatives you did of my work years ago?" Not locating them in my "everyday" file, I immediately located the file number of the architect on my "time machine" card file, opened a corresponding file in my "mine" and voila! There were negatives and an assortment of 8" x 10" prints and excellently preserved 4" x 5" color transparencies. Regarding the latter, a private secret: during the 1950s and into the 1960s, there existed another film producer, the Ansco Company of Binghamton, New York.

Ansco manufactured a color transparency film which has become a lifesaver! Whereas Eastman Kodak Co. had originally produced Kodachrome transparency film in all sizes, including 8" x 10", by the 1950s, it was replaced (except their 35 mm slide film) with Ektachrome. Apparently the "lifespan," chemically, of the coating was not favorable to those of us who, as with me, provide transparencies "forever." Most of my older 4" x 5" Ektachromes have become completely unusable. However, Ansco came to the rescue! In my old files devoted solely to transparencies, scattered together on many projects, I have located both films; that was because in the early years of Ansco's production I was not certain of the film's effectiveness. Therefore I took duplicate exposures, using both films – to my good fortune. Specifically in the previously described book on the architecture and interiors of the 1950s, almost all of my older color was produced from Ansco film.

Today in the late 1990s, I am exceedingly happy with the "performance" of my archives. But they function for a basic reason: they are 100% organized.

Soriano and Basque Shepherd during a walk with me, 1936

In 1997, Frank Gehry invited me to visit his workshop in Santa Monica, California. The occasion was informative, for although he had attained international prominence, I knew little of his background. My 1997 meeting with Gehry consisted of a tour of his "factory," as I best could describe the vast spaces which contained large scale models of much of Gehry's completed and "in progress" projects. What startled me was a demonstration of his computerized method of design executions, as operated by an associate. To me, never with any knowledge whatsoever of computer lore, that performance was sheer magic. I cannot begin to describe that experience, for my life had never been touched by the world of computers, except, I suppose, when I made reservations for a plane trip.

When I photographed Gehry's Steeves house in 1959, I had observed a touch of Soriano influence without recalling the previous Soriano-Gehry association. But Gehry's role in the international world of architecture has become legendary. Now my curiosity has

led to an analysis of how and why he either veered away or evolved in his practice towards a free-form structural emancipation. Occupying my own Soriano-designed home and studio, I, for one, am in a position to analyze. I sincerely regretted what I saw at that time as decades of flagrant departure from the architecture I had grown up with since my 1936 work with Richard Neutra, and I felt that something was "wrong."

But during our meeting and learning of his design directions I was impressed with Gehry's logic. At lunch he invited me to photograph his Guggenheim Bilbao Museum. Our conversation led to the subject of the proposed Disney Concert Hall. On tracing paper Gehry sketched out some of the circumstances involved. Finally, I suggested that if the public could have become aware of his design logic, there would be fewer denunciations of the project. Open-mindedness does not seem to be a universal human virtue. But possessing such a characteristic can lead to the minimalization of foregone conclusions; too frequently of a non-objective nature.

J. Paul Getty Center for the Fine Arts, 1997
Richard Meier, Brentwood, California, 1992–97

Gehry, pleased with my observation, phrased on the tracing paper sketches: "For the redemption of Julius Shulman," adding his signature. With my mind activated, I began to relate the stimulation to some of my photographic observations. In my studio one of the photographs of an 1880s house taken for the City of Los Angeles Cultural Heritage Board caught my attention. Suddenly I was drawn to the imaginative curvilinear forms; decorative, yet creating enclosed spaces which invited the viewer to explore. Did the architect foresee the reactions of the public in the nineteenth century almost into the twentieth? I have had that photograph shown in exhibitions. It appears as one of the most popular of the Carpenter Gothic houses in this area of Southern California.

Does not the design created by forming volumes as they meld into the total space hint at some precursor of Gehry's provocative configurations? But further, perhaps, pay tribute to the architect's daring to allow an exploration process to enter into his freedom of planning? How those thoughts and queries evoke a further challenge!

Acknowledgements

Acknowledgements

Like credits on the screen after a motion picture is completed, scores of names as the projection rolls on and on. Similarly, the cast in my life's projection, so numerous that I find it impossible to list all the "characters"! But my appreciation and respect for the vast multitude of associates, over what are now 62 years of participation in the world of architectural endeavors.

In retrospect I link together those pioneers who created the foundations of contemporary architecture in this area of the world: Gregory Ain, J.R. Davidson, R.M. Schindler, Raphael S. Soriano, and Richard J. Neutra.

I add another name, writer Esther McCoy, with whom I joined in recording a series of assignments. I continue to admire Esther's ability to seek out historical architectural subjects which resulted in successful stories for numerous publications.

On a totally removed expression of my association, I place my friendship with naturalist photographer Ansel Adams on a high plane of admiration. Adams and I had engaged in conversations involving our mutual concerns for environmental issues.

Adjacent to the aforementioned pioneers of modernism were the courageous editors of the few journals in the "early" years: George Sanderson and Thomas Creighton of *Progressive Architecture*; Douglas Haskell and Mary Jane Lightbown of the *Architectural Forum*, and Emerson Goble of the *Architectural Record*.

Together with the editors of the professional journals, I enjoyed the relationships with editors of other popular publications which realized the values that modernism could convey to their readers. I recall particularly my seventeen years of photographing for House and Garden magazine's editors, architecture with Will Mehlhorn, George Bailey for landscaping stories and also for the "better living" and decorating editors. Pursuing the recognition of the finest architectural gems, my *Life* magazine productions with Modern Living editor, Mary Hamman, resulted in greater acceptance by ever increasing modernism audiences.

Closer to home, my profound indebtedness to those reinforcing my early years of photography. In 1949, I engaged the services of a technician, Julius Frank, from Bremen, Germany. For ten years he processed my photographic assignments, making it possible for me to be relieved of a "double duty" existence. With his death in 1959, I was grateful when his wife Hildegard stepped into my organization, producing for 30 years prints which publishers appraised as the finest quality ever experienced in their presentations. Her continuation of Julius Franks' qualitative work made it possible for me to maintain the ever-increasing pace of assignments. My heartfelt respect and gratitude to the Franks!

Another gratitude-generating aspect of my current production is demonstrated by the services I receive from Custom Color, Inc., a processing organization which performed all my required printing after I dissolved my corporation in 1986. Under the direction of their CEO, Larry Lannin, Custom Color fulfills my publication requests for black and white and color prints; the primary requests for black and white printing are performed by their technician, Charlie Rivera. New paper and technical printing equipment make him the very best ever! And my recognition of the number of others at Custom Color is likewise an honored one; faultless and friendly relationship is duly recognized.

Although my work has been widely exhibited for many years, an entirely new and rare experience in my career was created by gallery owner Craig Krull in 1985. His was my introduction to an opportunity to offer my photographs to collectors, in ever increasing numbers, seeking quality black and white prints.

In 1994, Joseph Rosa of Columbia University School of Architecture produced, with thorough research of my archives, with designer Kim Shkapich, one of the most successful publications ever by Rizzoli, *A Constructed View: The Architectural Photography of Julius Shulman*. I am deeply indebted to him for expressing so brilliantly my life's productions in the pursuit of the photography of architecture and related designs. His selection of the title created for me a new perspective on my activities.

My fondest memories are attributed to the long years of association with the late Dan MacMasters, architectural editor of the Los Angeles Times Home Magazine. For countless years we traversed many areas of the world to produce stories. What a delightful companion, sharing our thoughts of architecture and observations on our life's experiences.

Finally, the 62 years of my career represent generations in the swift passage of time's calendar years. I wish that I could extend my acknowledgements to each and all – the scores upon scores of individuals ranging throughout my rewarding years in a profession which continues to invoke the realization that I am an extremely fortunate human being!

Front Cover:
Singleton House, 1960
Richard Neutra, Los Angeles, California, 1959

Back Cover:
Arango House, 1973
John Lautner, Acapulco, Mexico, 1973

Julius Shulman's photography is represented by
Craig Krull Gallery
Bergomot Station, 2525 Michigan Avenue
USA-Santa Monica, California 90404

© 1998 Benedikt Taschen Verlag GmbH
Hohenzollernring 53, D-50672 Köln

© for all photographs:
Julius Shulman, Los Angeles, California

Designed by:
Peter Gössel, Bremen
Cover designed by:
Peter Gössel, Bremen; Angelika Taschen, Cologne

Printed in Germany
ISBN 3-8228-7204-0